My New York Sketchbook
version 2

Kyoko Mitsufuji / Megumi Uesugi

SANSHUSHA

音声ダウンロード＆ストリーミングサービス（無料）のご案内

http://www.sanshusha.co.jp/onsei/isbn/9784384334449/

本書の音声データは、上記アドレスよりダウンロードおよびストリーミング再生ができます。ぜひご利用ください。

■NY 現地取材の特典映像について

ニューヨークの風景を中心としたイメージ映像（3 分程度）10 本、インタビュー映像（5 分～8 分程度）4 本の計 14 本をご用意しております。
動画ファイルの項目は以下の通りです。

- 01 Grand Central Terminal 〈UNIT 1、UNIT 13 などに関連〉
- 02 Streets and Avenues 〈UNIT 3 などに関連〉
- 03 Subway 〈UNIT 5 に関連〉
- 04 Food 〈UNIT 7 などに関連〉
- 05 Historical Buildings and Skyscrapers 〈UNIT 8 などに関連〉
- 06 Brooklyn 〈UNIT 9 などに関連〉
- 07 Musicals 〈UNIT 12 に関連〉
- 08 Markets 〈UNIT 14 に関連〉
- 09 Parks 〈UNIT 16 などに関連〉
- 10 Art & Museums 〈UNIT 17 に関連〉
- 11 Interview (1) Rise Endo 〈A Japanese in NY [1] p. 28 に関連〉
- 12 Interview (2) Kenichiro Sano 〈A Japanese in NY [2] p. 50 に関連〉
- 13 Interview (3) Yuta Takeda 〈A Japanese in NY [3] p. 72 に関連〉
- 14 Interview (4) Masayo Hosono 〈A Japanese in NY [4] p. 94 に関連〉

01～11 は
こちらから↓

＊動画 01～11 は下記 URL の YouTube 専用チャンネルでご覧いただけます。
https://www.youtube.com/channel/UCQnmes41MglcPmRZuD-ixUw
（チャンネル名 MyNewYorkSketchbook_ver2_SANSHUSHA）

＊動画 12～14 につきましては、ご採用クラスの先生へのご案内となります。

■ 写真提供

pp. 4, 5, 8, 12, 16, 24, 28, 30, 34, 38, 42, 46, 50, 52, 56 (left), 60, 64, 68, 72, 74, 78, 82, 86, 90, 94 © 上杉恵美 〔肖像は本人の許諾を得て掲載〕

p. 37 © iStockphoto.com/GMVozd

p. 67 © iStockphoto.com/Chiyacat

p. 20 © iStockphoto.com/amriphoto

p. 23 (above) © iStockphoto.com/stefanobesana

p. 23 (below) © iStockphoto.com/AlbertPego

p. 56 (right) © iStockphoto.com/thall

p. 85 © iStockphoto.com/josiephos

p. 93 (left) © iStockphoto.com/Moncherie

p. 93 (right) © iStockphoto.com/Smileus

■ A Japanese in New York (pp. 28, 50, 72, 94) について
掲載されている記事は 2013 年 5 月の取材に基づいています。

はじめに

　『My New York Sketchbook』旧版が出版されたのは、今から13年前のことです。著者らは2回に渡って渡米し、当時のニューヨークを取材しました。そして旧版が完成するちょうどその頃、ニューヨークのツインタワーが無残にもテロリストによって破壊されるという事実を、テレビの映像を通して知ることになったのです。愛すべきニューヨークが憎しみの標的になったことは、我々はもちろん、世界中の多くの人々の心に傷跡として残りました。

　あれから10年以上が経過し、ニューヨークは再び活気に満ちた姿を取り戻したように思えます。新版を出版するにあたり取材で訪れた2013年5月、街は春の花が一斉に咲いてエネルギーに溢れ、さまざまな国から来た人々でにぎわっていました。

　この新版の主人公は、**Rika Tanaka** という現代美術を学ぶ大学生です。彼女が10か月に渡るニューヨーク滞在で得た知識や経験を、日本にいる恩師の **May J. Sato** 先生に英語でレポートする、という形式です。旧版と同じく本書は、さまざまなテーマのもとに物語が展開する **Reading Passage**、本文の理解を確かめる **Comprehension**、本文で使われている慣用表現を短文の中で練習する **Useful Expressions**、本文に関連した実用会話を聞き取り、会話の練習としても使える **Listening**、あたかも本物のニューヨークが体験できるかのように工夫された **Activity** からなっています。また、旧版でも好評だった **A Japanese in NY** では、現在ニューヨークで活躍する4人の日本人が生き生きと暮らす様子を知ることができます。ニューヨークの街角をユニークな目で描写したコラム [**New York** の街角から] とともにお楽しみください。

　なお、本書には、現地で録画したニューヨークの風景と、**A Japanese in NY** で紹介している4人のインタビュー映像を見ることができる特典がついています。どうぞ楽しみながらご活用ください。

　本書の出版にあたっては、遠藤梨世さん、佐野健一郎さん、竹田雄太さん、細野雅世さん、土江亨JTB NY支店長の皆様をはじめ、たくさんの方々のご協力を得ました。心よりお礼申し上げます。

　本書が皆さんの英語学習に役立つことを期待するとともに、いつかニューヨークを訪れてみたい！と皆さんに感じていただければ、著者としてこれほど嬉しいことはありません。

2015年2月

著者

CONTENTS

- **8** **UNIT 1** Arriving in New York
  さあ、ニューヨークだ！

- **12** **UNIT 2** Visiting an Apartment in Chelsea
  チェルシーのアパートを訪ねる

- **16** **UNIT 3** Streets and Avenues in Manhattan
  「ストリート」と「アベニュー」

- **20** **UNIT 4** Discovering the American Heart
  アメリカの心に出会って

- **24** **UNIT 5** Getting Around by Subway
  地下鉄を乗りこなす

- **28** A Japanese in NY [1]　Rise Endo
- **29** コラム New York の街角から [1]　ニューヨークのタクシー

- **30** **UNIT 6** College Life
  ニューヨークの学生生活

- **34** **UNIT 7** Food in New York
  ニューヨーク 食探検

- **38** **UNIT 8** Skyscrapers are the Landmarks
  高層ビルは道しるべ

- **42** **UNIT 9** Dazzling Brooklyn
  活気づくブルックリン

- **46** **UNIT 10** Email from the Teacher (1)
  ニューヨークへのメッセージ (1)

- **50** A Japanese in NY [2]　Kenichiro Sano
- **51** コラム New York の街角から [2]　パブリック・アート

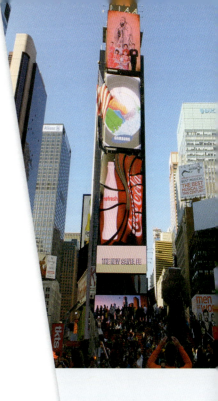

- 52　**UNIT 11**　Friends from Different Countries
  異文化コミュニケーションを楽しむ

- 56　**UNIT 12**　Musicals on a Shoestring
  安くミュージカルを見る方法

- 60　**UNIT 13**　Viva Grand Central Terminal!
  100年の時を超えて

- 64　**UNIT 14**　Markets are Fun
  マーケットは最高！

- 68　**UNIT 15**　September 11 Memorial
  追悼の地を訪れて

- 72 73　**A Japanese in NY [3]**　Yuta Takeda
  コラム New Yorkの街角から [3]　ベンダー

- 74　**UNIT 16**　Central Park & City Marathon
  セントラルパークとシティマラソン

- 78　**UNIT 17**　Contemporary Art in New York
  ニューヨークは現代美術の宝庫

- 82　**UNIT 18**　Christmas in New York
  ニューヨークのクリスマス

- 86　**UNIT 19**　Email from the Teacher (2)
  ニューヨークへのメッセージ（2）

- 90　**UNIT 20**　Goodbye, New York
  さよなら、ニューヨーク！

- 94 95　**A Japanese in NY [4]**　Masayo Hosono
  コラム New Yorkの街角から [4]　NYでスポーツ観戦！

本文の登場人物

Rika	NY の大学に 10 か月留学する日本人女子大学生。
May J. Sato	Rika が在籍する日本の大学の英語教師。
Oliver	Rika の父親の友人。New Jersey 在住のアメリカ人。
Sara	Oliver の妻。
Angie	Parsons The New School for Design に通う女子学生。香港出身。
Jonathan	Angie のボーイフレンド。

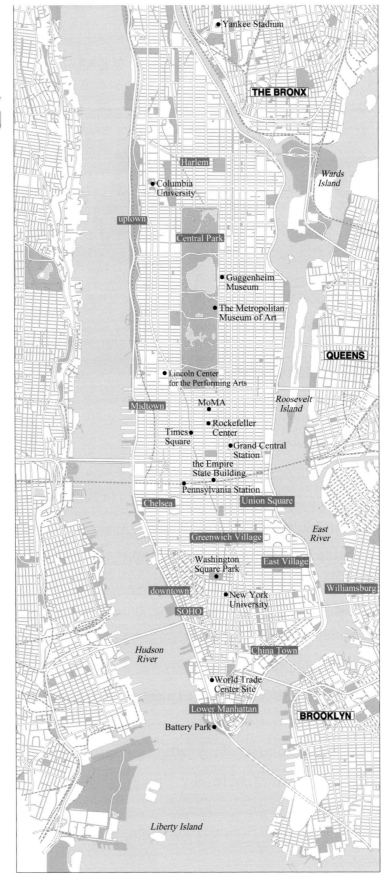

UNIT 1 Arriving in New York

さあ、ニューヨークだ！

Rika's Report

    I have arrived in New York—the place I have dreamed of coming to study in for so long. I am going to report on various aspects of this city and peoples' lives during my ten-month stay here. Let me get started with how my first day went.

    The flight from Tokyo was quite smooth, and I landed at JFK safely. I was a bit nervous at Immigration, but the immigration officer's "Good luck, young lady!" really cheered me up. I decided to take the airport bus, which goes straight into the heart of Manhattan. Honestly, I was tempted to take a taxi because my heavy suitcase and huge backpack were killing me. But the twenty dollar bus fare seemed a real bargain.

    My first bus ride in this city, however, did not go as expected. I was so absorbed in the unfamiliar view of Queens and fascinated by the energy of Manhattan that I didn't realize the bus was heading for a different terminal. I was going to meet Oliver, a friend of my father, at Penn Station—not Grand Central. I could not have made a mistake because the girl selling bus tickets at JFK told me this was the right bus.

    On the bus I was totally at a loss and feeling helpless. But I finally plucked up the courage to tell the driver, "Excuse me, but I wanted to go to Penn Station." The driver, who I presumed was an immigrant from South America by his accent, said with a big smile, "Don't worry, Miss." Then he called a free shuttle bus at the next stop, which took me to the right destination. What a relief! The best way to survive in New York is to just ask.

　I met Oliver in front of the famous Madison Square Garden, where Penn Station is located on the ground floor. We had not seen each other since he and his wife Sara left Japan six months ago. "Hi, Rika. Welcome to New York," he smiled. "Great to see you, Oliver." My eyes got blurry with tears.

　I am staying with them in New Jersey this week. Next Monday, they will help me move into the university dorm.　　　　　　　　　　　　　　(369 words)

Notes

▶ p. 8
- l. 4　**JFK**「ジョン・F・ケネディ国際空港」
- l. 5　**Immigration**「入国審査」
- l. 7　**be tempted to ...**「... したい誘惑にかられる」
- l. 9　**bargain**「かなりお得なもの」
- l. 10　**be absorbed in ...**「... に夢中になる」
- l. 11　**Queens**「クィーンズ地区」
- l. 13　**Penn Station**「ペンシルバニア駅」1日600本もの列車が発着する巨大なターミナル。
- l. 13　**Grand Central**「グランドセントラル駅」（詳細は Unit 13 参照）
- l. 16　**totally at a loss**「まったくどうしてよいかわからない」
- l. 16　**pluck up the courage to**「勇気をふりしぼって ... する」

▶ p. 9
- l. 2　**presume**「推測する」
- l. 6　**Madison Square Garden**「マジソン・スクエア・ガーデン」地上のアリーナは、バスケットボールやアイスホッケーのホーム試合場、ロックコンサート会場としても有名。
- l. 9　**got blurry**「ぼやけた」

TIPS

NYには、JFK、Newark、La Guardia の3つの空港がある。マンハッタンへはタクシー、バス、地下鉄のどれかを使うが、ホテルまで運んでくれるシャトルバスも運行されているので、よく調べてから行くとよい。

I Comprehension

次の各文が本文の内容と合っている場合は **T**、間違っている場合は **F** を選びなさい。

1. T / F　The girl selling bus tickets at JFK gave Rika the correct information.
2. T / F　Rika had to pay extra money for the bus to Penn Station.
3. T / F　Rika had known Oliver before she came to New York.

II Useful Expressions

（　）の中に適語を入れ、それぞれの和文に合う英文を作りなさい。

1. 友達からの温かいメッセージで元気になった。
   The warm message from my friend (　　　　　) me (　　　　).

2. 英語でそれを何と言ってよいかわからず、途方に暮れてしまった。
   I had no idea how to say it in English, so I felt (　　　　　) (　　　　) (　　　　)
   (　　　　).

3. 勇気をふりしぼって先生に話しかけたら、笑顔で答えてくれた。
   I (　　　　) (　　　　) (　　　　) (　　　　　　) (　　　　) talk to the teacher. Then, he answered me with a smile.

III Listening

ダイアローグを聞き、空所を埋めなさい。

—Rika talks to a girl selling bus tickets at the bus station.

Rika: Excuse me, but (　　　　) (　　　　) (　　　　) (　　　　) (　　　　) to Manhattan?

Girl: Yeah. The bus is arriving (　　　　) (　　　　) (　　　　). Do you want a ticket? It's twenty dollars.

Rika: Yes, please. Does the bus go to Penn Station?

Girl: Yes, it does. (　　　　　) (　　　　　) the bus. See the yellow one?

Rika: Thanks. Good-bye.

Girl: (　　　　　) your stay. I'm sure you'll love New York!

Activity

下の図は、Rika が渡米する頃のニューヨークの天気予報です。各曜日の天気の説明として適当なものを (a) ～ (d) から選び、(　) に入れてみましょう。

Mon.	Tues.	Wed.	Thurs.
High: 55°F Low: 37°F Humidity: 48%	High: 50°F Low: 36°F Humidity: 70%	High: 45°F Low: 33°F Humidity: 50%	High: 58°F Low: 40°F Humidity: 35%
(　)	(　)	(　)	(　)

Notes: F = Fahrenheit（華氏）

* Celsius（摂氏）= 5/9（F − 32）

参考に次の数値を覚えておくとよい。

60°F = 約 16℃　　50°F = 約 10℃　　40°F = 約 4℃　　30°F = 約 -1℃

(a) Mostly sunny. Low humidity.

(b) Partly cloudy. Highs in the mid 50s.

(c) Partly cloudy with a chance of showers.

(d) Mostly cloudy. Lows in the lower 30s.

UNIT 2

Visiting an Apartment in Chelsea

チェルシーのアパートを訪ねる

Rika's Report

I moved into the university dorm a week ago. My life in New York has become more settled over the past two weeks.

During my stay at Oliver's, I was introduced to a student from Hong Kong whose name is Angie. Today I visited her apartment in Chelsea. It's on West 15th
5 Street close to Greenwich Village. Angie is studying architectural design at Parsons The New School for Design not far from her apartment. It has a bedroom, a kitchen with a small dining space, and a bathroom with a shower. It's not a big apartment but looks clean and cozy to live in.

Angie, her friend Jonathan and I had dinner in her tiny dining room. "What are
10 you going to do in New York, Rika?" asked Jonathan. I said, "My main interest here is to study contemporary art. But I'm interested in many other things, too." Jonathan said, "You're lucky to live in New York. It's got everything—music, art, sports, restaurants, exciting people and diverse cultures." Angie nodded in agreement saying, "Look what I got for dinner tonight! Chinese noodles, Japanese
15 sushi, Jewish bagels and Italian tiramisu for dessert."

After dinner, we walked out of her apartment to get some fresh air. There was a larger crowd in the evening than in the daytime in Chelsea. It looked like a multicultural neighborhood with different races, ethnic groups and social classes. There is a taste of artistry and dynamism in this town.

 According to Jonathan, Chelsea has undergone a lot of renovation recently. Chelsea Piers on 23rd Street near the Hudson River has a huge sports complex for skating, bowling, swimming and golfing for sports-loving families as well as individuals to unwind after work. Angie said, "You can find a lot of interesting things at Chelsea Market. I also love going to small galleries here."

 "Do you like American literature, Rika?" asked Jonathan. "If you do and want to feel nostalgic, Hotel Chelsea is worth a peek because Mark Twain, Thomas Wolfe and Tennessee Williams used to stay there when writing their masterpieces." I thought I would definitely go visit that hotel while I'm in New York! (359 words)

Notes

▶ p. 12
- *l.* 5 **Greenwich Village**「グリニッチ・ビレッジ」別名 Village とも呼ばれ、地価の安かった昔は芸術家が多く住んだ。
- *l.* 5 **Parsons The New School for Design**「パーソンズ美術大学」グリニッチ・ビレッジにあるこの大学はマーク・ジェイコブズやダナ・キャランなど有名なデザイナーを輩出していることで有名。
- *l.* 11 **contemporary art**「現代美術」
- *l.* 13 **diverse**「多様な」

▶ p. 13
- *l.* 3 **a taste of ...**「... の雰囲気」
- *l.* 5 **Chelsea Piers**「チェルシー・ピアーズ」1995 年に、もともとハドソン川埠頭だったところを改造してできた巨大なスポーツセンター。
- *l.* 5 **sports complex**「複合スポーツ施設」
- *l.* 7 **unwind**「くつろぐ」
- *l.* 8 **Chelsea Market**「チェルシー・マーケット」W.(West)15th St./9th Ave. にある倉庫を改造したショッピングモール。
- *l.* 10 **Hotel Chelsea**「チェルシー・ホテル」W.23rd St. にある、1884 年に建てられたホテル。マーク・トウェインなどのアメリカ文学の作家たちが愛したことで有名。現在改装中で 2015 年に再オープンの予定。
- *l.* 10 **worth a peek**「見るに値する」

TIPS

かつては荒廃していたチェルシーだが、現在では倉庫を改造した新しいタイプのギャラリーや、食材店、ケーキ屋、アンティークショップなどが連なるショッピング・モールを中心に、NY の人気エリアになっている。

I Comprehension

次の各文が本文の内容と合っている場合は T、間違っている場合は F を選びなさい。

1. T / F   Rika and Angie are going to share an apartment.
2. T / F   Angie majors in architectural design at New York University.
3. T / F   You can find a mixture of the old and new in Chelsea.

II Useful Expressions

(   ) の中に適語を入れ、それぞれの和文に合う英文を作りなさい。

1. 私は、明山大学で心理学を専攻しています。
   I (   ) (   ) psychology at Meizan University.
2. その古い図書館は現在改築中です。
   The old library is (   ) (   ) right now.
3. 15丁目の新しいカフェはぜひ覗いてみてください。
   The new cafe on 15th Street is (   ) (   ) (   ).

III Listening

ダイアローグを聞き、空所を埋めなさい。

—Rika, Angie and Jonathan talk about their schools and majors.

Jonathan: (   ) (   ) (   ) (   ) (   ) study in New York, Rika?

Rika: I'm interested in studying contemporary art.

Jonathan: That (   ) interesting. I (   ) (   ) computer science.

Rika: What do you study, Angie?

Angie: I study industrial design.

Rika: Is your school near here?

Angie: Yes, I can (   ) (   ) school from my apartment.

Unit 2

Activity

２つのアパートの間取りと条件を見て、不動産屋のアンケートに答えてみましょう。

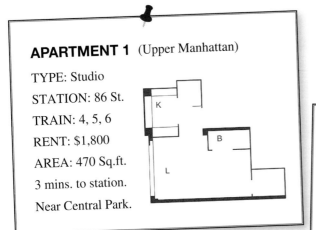

APARTMENT 1 (Upper Manhattan)
TYPE: Studio
STATION: 86 St.
TRAIN: 4, 5, 6
RENT: $1,800
AREA: 470 Sq.ft.
3 mins. to station.
Near Central Park.

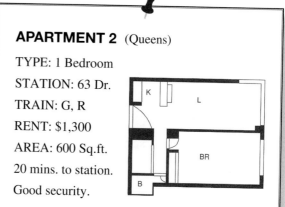

APARTMENT 2 (Queens)
TYPE: 1 Bedroom
STATION: 63 Dr.
TRAIN: G, R
RENT: $1,300
AREA: 600 Sq.ft.
20 mins. to station.
Good security.

NY ABC REAL ESTATE

Put checks (✓) in the boxes you choose.

1. Which type of apartment do you like better?
   ☐ Studio   ☐ 1 Bedroom

2. Which of the below are most important to you? (Check three)
   ☐ Convenience
   ☐ Rent
   ☐ Size
   ☐ Location
   ☐ Safety

3. Therefore, I like ☐ APARTMENT 1 ／ ☐ APARTMENT 2.

UNIT 3
Streets and Avenues in Manhattan

「ストリート」と「アベニュー」

Rika's Report

After a month here in New York, or "the Big Apple" as it is also known, I feel that I am getting used to it. So today I would like to report about the "streets" and "avenues" in New York City.

Manhattan Island is bounded by the Hudson River to the west and the East River to the east. The thin, long island, stretching from south to north, is only four kilometers in width. The entire area almost equals the inner area of the Yamanote Line in Tokyo. The two hundred and twenty streets, numbered in order from south to north, run from east to west. They are vertically crossed by thirteen avenues stretching towards the north from the southern part of the island.

This grid-style layout was designed by city planners back in the early 19th century. Broadway Street, home to various famous musicals, still retains its original scenery from before the city planning. Central Park is bounded by Fifth Avenue, Eighth Avenue, 59th Street and 110th Street. It's literally the "center" of Manhattan.

If you walk down a street, you come across street and avenue signs at every big crossing. Such signs help you to easily find where you are.

But when you are lost in this city, people often give you directions using the word "block." Soon after I arrived here, I was opening up a map on the street to find Strand, a famous bookstore. An old man who happened to pass by kindly told me, "Go straight for three blocks from here. You will find it on the right." Then, the other day, I was walking along Sixth Avenue and was asked by an Italian tourist how he could get to Macy's. I proudly answered like a New Yorker. "Walk down this street for three blocks. You will find a big building on your right. That's Macy's."

I like Sixth Avenue best because there I can find my favorite park, Bryant Park, next to the Public Library and Kinokuniya Book Store, where I often stop by. As for the streets, there are just too many to remember!

(352 words)

Notes

▶ p. 16
- *l. 1* **the Big Apple** 「ビッグアップル」ニューヨーク市の愛称。その由来には諸説がある。
- *l. 4* **be bounded by ...** 「...（の境界）に接している」
- *l. 8* **vertically crossed** 「垂直に交差している」
- *l. 10* **grid-style layout** 「格子状の設計」
- *l. 11* **home to ...** 「...が沢山集まることで知られる場所」
- *l. 15* **come across ...** 「...に出会う」

▶ p. 17
- *l. 3* **Strand** 「ストランド」E.(East) 12th St./Broadway の交差点角にある1927年創立の老舗書店。
- *l. 6* **Macy's** 「メイシーズ」ミッドタウンにある有名デパート。ブランド物から手頃な価格の物まで幅広い品揃えで人気がある。
- *l. 9* **Bryant Park** 「ブライアントパーク」公共図書館に隣接する庭園と噴水が美しい公園。
- *l. 10* **Public Library** 「ニューヨーク公共図書館」5th Ave. 沿いにある世界屈指の規模の図書館。クラシックな建築とライオン像が目印。
- *l. 10* **Kinokuniya Book Store** 「紀伊國屋書店」ブライアントパークの向かい側にある日本の老舗書店のニューヨーク支店。

Tips

マンハッタンの東西を走る 1st St. 以北の Street は、南北を走る 5th Ave. を境に East と West に分かれており、建物の住所には通りの名前が含まれている。マンハッタンを移動する際は、通りの名前が一番のナビゲーターである。

I Comprehension

次の各文が本文の内容と合っている場合は **T**、間違っている場合は **F** を選びなさい。

1. T / F　The size of Manhattan almost equals the inner area of the Yamanote Line.
2. T / F　The grid-style streets and avenues were designed in the late 18th century.
3. T / F　In New York, it is easy to tell anybody directions using the word "block."

II Useful Expressions

（　）の中に適語を入れ、それぞれの和文に合う英文を作りなさい。

1. 中之島は、堂島川と土佐堀川に挟まれています。
   Nakanoshima is (　　　) (　　　) the Doshima River and the Tosabori River.

2. この地図があれば、駅までの道が簡単にわかります。
   This map (　　　) (　　　) (　　　) easily find the way to the station.

3. 2ブロックほど歩いて行くと、右側に東京駅があります。
   If you walk for two blocks, you will find Tokyo Station (　　　) (　　　) (　　　).

III Listening

ダイアローグを聞き、空所を埋めなさい。

　　—A stranger talks to Rika on the street.

Man: Excuse me, do you know (　　) (　　) get to Bryant Park?

Rika: It's on Sixth Avenue next to the Public Library.

Man: (　　) (　　) (　　) (　　) where we are on this map?

Rika: (*Pointing to the map*) We are right here on Seventh Avenue, so if you walk a (　　) (　　) from here, you will get to Bryant Park.

Man: (　　) (　　) (　　) Japan or Korea?

Rika: I'm from Tokyo, Japan.

Man: Your English is excellent!

Rika: Thank you.

Activity

現在地から地図を見ながら次の指示に従って進み、**Riverside Park (Destination)** にたどり着いてみましょう。次に、**Cafe Lalo** への道順を英語で言ってみましょう。

(1) Go straight along Broadway for 3 blocks.

(2) You'll see Zabar's on your left.

(3) Turn left just before Zabar's.

(4) Go straight for 2 blocks.

(5) You'll see Riverside Park across the street.

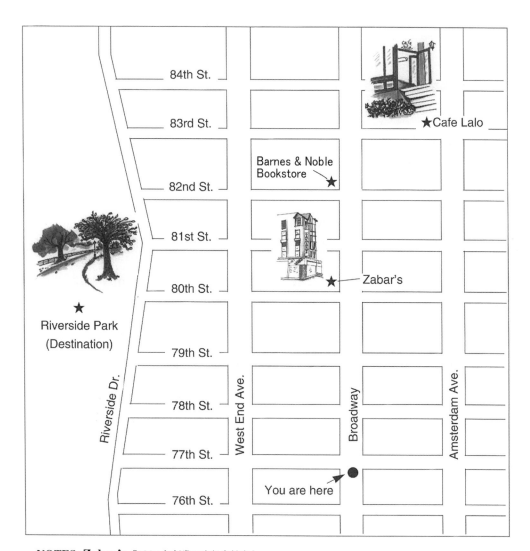

NOTES: Zabar's「1934年創業の高級食材店」

UNIT 4

Discovering the American Heart

アメリカの心に出会って

Rika's Report

This morning, I got a sudden call from Oliver and Sara. I was out late with my friends last night, so I was still fast asleep. Oliver shouted over the phone, "Rika, you can't waste such a fine weekend like this. Get out of bed and let's go see the Statue of Liberty and Ellis Island by ferry!"

The three of us took the subway to Battery Park at the southern tip of Manhattan. People were waiting for ferries, listening to the seagulls squawking in the sky. I hate boat rides, but this one was an exception. From the rear deck of the ferry, we could feel the Atlantic breeze and see the skyscrapers in Lower Manhattan gradually fading away from our sight. Oliver was right! We can enjoy this only on such a clear morning. When we finally lost sight of Manhattan, the gigantic Statue of Liberty with her overwhelming dignity appeared before our eyes.

I was wondering why we are still attracted to the Statue. Why does it remain the symbol of America? It has been more than one hundred years since it was presented by the people of France to the United States. I think I found the answer on Ellis Island which we visited next.

According to the brochure, the Immigration Museum on Ellis Island used to be the center for immigration processing from the late 19th to the early 20th century. More than twelve million immigrants were drawn here from various parts of the world. The inspection of such immigrants before their entry into the mainland began in 1892 and continued through 1954.

5   Sara said, "About one in three Americans has an ancestor coming through here. My ancestors came from Scotland, Poland and Italy. I heard they had a hard time sailing to America. The Statue of Liberty always welcomed such people—looking for hope and new dreams—with infinite warmness and generosity."

On the "Wall of Honor" outside the main building, you can see the names of
10 the immigrants etched into steel plates. Sara said she would be so excited if she found her family name Kotarsky on one of them.

(357 words)

Notes

▶ p. 20
- l. 2 **fast asleep**「ぐっすり眠っている」
- l. 4 **Statue of Liberty**「自由の女神」
- l. 4 **Ellis Island**「エリス島」自由の女神のあるリバティー島とともにフェリーで立ち寄ることができる。移民博物館には、ここを経てアメリカに入国した人々の写真、記録フィルム、持ち物、当時のパスポートなどが展示されている。
- l. 5 **Battery Park**「バッテリー・パーク」マンハッタンの南端、ここからフェリーに乗船する。
- l. 6 **squawking**「鳥などがやかましく鳴く」
- l. 8 **Lower Manhattan**「ロウアー・マンハッタン」マンハッタンの南端に位置する地域。ウォール・ストリートなどの金融街で有名。
- l. 9 **fade away**「徐々に消える」
- l. 11 **overwhelming**「圧倒される」
- l. 12 **be attracted to ...**「...に惹きつけられる」

▶ p. 21
- l. 8 **infinite**「限りない」
- l. 10 **etched into**「(銅版など) に刻まれる」

Tips

無料で自由の女神を見る方法として、マンハッタンとスタテン島を結ぶ通勤用の Staten Island Ferry がある。海にぽっかり浮かぶ自由の女神の遠景や、遠くにだんだん小さくなっていくマンハッタンの高層ビル群を見ることができる。

I Comprehension

次の各文が本文の内容と合っている場合は **T**、間違っている場合は **F** を選びなさい。

1. T / F　The Statue of Liberty was a gift from France.
2. T / F　Nearly half of Americans have ancestors who entered America through Ellis Island.
3. T / F　Sara's ancestors came from Scotland, Germany and Italy.

II Useful Expressions

(　) の中に適語を入れ、それぞれの和文に合う英文を作りなさい。

1. 休暇を寝て過ごすなんてもったいないですよ。
   You shouldn't (　　　　　) your vacation just sleeping.

2. 健二は、ジムで会った美しい女性に惹かれた。
   Kenji (　　　) (　　　　　) (　　　　) the beautiful woman he saw at the gym.

3. 私は、この国の言語と習慣に慣れるのに苦労した。
   I (　　　) (　　　) (　　　　) (　　　　　) getting used to the language and customs in this country.

III Listening

ダイアローグを聞き、空所を埋めなさい。

—Rika, Oliver and Sara are visiting the Statue of Liberty.

Rika: Have you been to the top of the Statue of Liberty?
Sara: Never! To be honest, this is (　　　) (　　　　) (　　　) getting so close to the Statue.
Rika: I see. It's like I've (　　　　) (　　　) (　　　) the top of Tokyo Tower.
Sara: Yeah, this is the place for tourists.
Rika: Do you know (　　　　) (　　　　) you can go?
Sara: I think you can climb up to the crown. It (　　　　) (　　　) a gorgeous view from up there.

Activity

「自由の女神」クイズ：正解を選びましょう。

Q1 How tall is the Statue of Liberty from the ground to the tip of the flame?
 (A) About 63m
 (B) About 93m
 (C) About 123m

Q2 How many windows are there in the crown of the Statue?
 (A) 10   (B) 18   (C) 25

Q3 What main material makes up the Statue of the Liberty?
 (A) Copper   (B) Stone   (C) Platinum

Q4 What is written on the tablet which the Statue holds in her left hand?
 (A) The birthday of the woman who is thought to be the model of the Statue
 (B) The date of American Independence
 (C) The date when the Statue was completed

Q5 Which direction does the Statue face?
 (A) Southeast
 (B) North
 (C) Northwest

参照：www.nps.gov/stli/historyculture/statue-statistics.htm
www.nps.gov/stli/faqs.htm

UNIT 5 Getting Around by Subway

地下鉄を乗りこなす

Rika's Report

New York subways are cleaner and safer than I thought. Their bad reputation is something of the past and I cannot survive here without them. The platforms are old and not spacious, but quite safe in the daytime when there are many people commuting or traveling. Although you should not stand alone on the platform at
5　midnight, the subway is convenient and easy to use, and it takes you quickly to various parts of the city.

There are many ways to ride the subway in New York. You can buy a single ticket or get a MetroCard. Both of them are available from vending machines which you can easily find near the entrance to the platform. If you are a frequent subway
10　rider or visiting here for more than a week, the Unlimited Ride MetroCard is handy. You pay thirty dollars for seven days and it is more economical than buying a single ride ticket, which costs you two dollars and seventy-five cents for every ride. With an Unlimited Ride MetroCard, you get free transfers when switching from one line to another, or even to a bus line. What is more, you can travel anywhere
15　and as many times as you want within the same day.

Next, let me give some advice on how to use the subway. Once you get a card, you will swipe it at the turnstile. If the turnstile screen says "Go," you can go through, but do not get frightened when you see the sign, "Please swipe again." The art of swiping is— not to swipe too fast, but not too slowly!

You should also be careful not to go through the wrong entrance. Many stations have separate entrances to uptown and downtown. It is a bit of a shock if you notice you are heading in the opposite direction in the middle of your ride.

Finally, the ads placed inside trains are interesting, too. Just yesterday on the train, I saw a campaign ad for preventing domestic violence. There were some photos of women who were hurt and beaten by their husbands or boyfriends. It certainly shows us the dark side of New York City. (362 words)

Notes
▶ **p. 24**
- *l. 7* **single ticket** 「一回で使い切る片道切符」
- *l. 8* **available from ...** 「...で手に入る」
- *l. 10* **Unlimited Ride MetroCard** 「乗り放題メトロカード」決められた期間内であれば、乗り放題のプリペイド・カード。
- *l. 11* **handy** 「便利な」

▶ **p. 25**
- *l. 1* **swipe** 「さっと（カードを）通す」
- *l. 1* **turnstile** 「自動改札の回転出入り口」
- *l. 2* **get frightened** 「怖がる」
- *l. 2* **the art of ...** 「...のコツ」
- *l. 5* **uptown** NY の地下鉄で、現在自分がいる位置より北の方角をアップタウンと呼ぶ。
- *l. 5* **downtown** 同じく南の方角をダウンタウンと呼ぶ。
- *l. 8* **domestic violence** 「家庭内暴力」

Tips

NY の地下鉄は時々工事が行われ、必ずしも地図通りでないこともあるので注意が必要。また、休日には大幅な運行の変更があるので、駅構内の掲示をよく見ること。

I Comprehension

次の各文が本文の内容と合っている場合は T、間違っている場合は F を選びなさい。

1. T / F　In New York, many people use the subway for commuting and traveling.
2. T / F　It is more economical to buy an Unlimited Ride MetroCard than a single ticket if you stay for more than a week.
3. T / F　The art of swiping is to swipe as slowly as possible.

II Useful Expressions

(　) の中に適語を入れ、それぞれの和文に合う英文を作りなさい。

1. キャンパスは、思ったよりずっと大きかった。
   The campus is much (　　　　) (　　　　) (　　　　) (　　　　).
2. 最近の若者にとって、スマートフォンは必需品です。
   These days, young people cannot (　　　　) (　　　　) a smartphone.
3. 小冊子は、ロビーの受付で手に入れることができます。
   The brochures (　　) (　　　　　) at the reception desk in the lobby.

III Listening

ダイアローグを聞き、空所を埋めなさい。

　—Rika buys a MetroCard at the subway ticket booth.

Rika: (　　　) (　　　) a seven-day Unlimited Ride Card, please.
Man: Thirty dollars.
Rika: (　　　) (　　　) (　　　) (　　　) at which station I should change to the B or Q Line?
Man: (　　　　) at 14th Street on Sixth Avenue.
Rika: (　　　) (　　) (　　　) a subway map?
Man: Sure. Here it is.
Rika: Thanks.

Activity

地下鉄のスケジュール変更を知らせる掲示を読み、1〜4のうち内容が合っているものには T、合っていないものには F を（ ）に書き入れましょう。

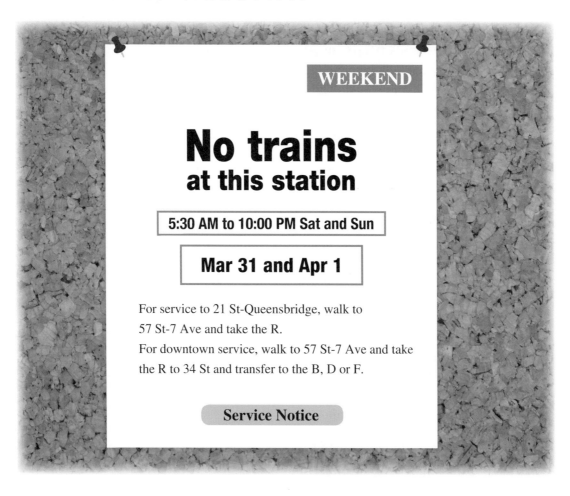

1. (　) Trains will run from 5:30 p.m. to 10:00 p.m. on March 31st and April 1st.
2. (　) If you go to 21st St-Queensbridge, you will have to take the R (Line).
3. (　) If you go downtown, you will have to change trains at 34th St.
4. (　) You are at 57th St-7th Ave now.

A Japanese in New York [1]

Rise Endo
—Chief Designer at Yabu Pushelberg

遠藤さんはNYに18年間住んでいます。現在はYabu Pushelbergという建築デザイン会社でチーフ・デザイナーとして活躍しています。会社はシンガービルという歴史的建造物の中にあり、会議室やカフェテリア、プロジェクトに使う本や雑誌が詰まった図書コーナーもあります。遠藤さんはアジアやヨーロッパにあるホテルや小売店、一般・集合住宅など、多くのプロジェクトを手がけてきました。現在は、マンハッタンに近く、芸術家が多く住むウィリアムズバークで暮らしています。

英語のナレーションを聞き、1～5のアンダーラインの箇所に当てはまるものをa～cの中から選びなさい。

1. Rise worked for some _____ firms before joining her present firm.
   a. insurance   b. computer   c. architectural

2. Their office is in the Singer Building which was built in _____.
   a. 1902   b. 1912   c. 1920

3. Their projects are around the world including Asia, Europe, and one in _____.
   a. Japan   b. Jordan   c. Sudan

4. Not only artists but also the _____ live in Williamsburg.
   a. young and old   b. young and rich   c. young and hip

5. Beacon's Closet sells second-hand _____.
   a. cars   b. clothes   c. furniture

Notes

Parsons School of Design Unit 2 では Parsons The New School for Design になっているが、名称が変わったため。
Yabu Pushelberg ヤブ・プッシェルバーグ。NYやトロントにオフィスを持ち、世界中の一流ホテルやレストラン、小売店の内装を手掛ける、今もっとも注目されるデザインオフィス。
Singer Building シンガービル。20世紀はじめにミシン製造会社シンガーの本社として建てられた。NYにある歴史的建造物のひとつ。
façade ファサード。建物の正面。
residences 戸建て住宅
Barneys New York バーニーズ・ニューヨーク。ハイセンスなスペシャリティストアとして、日本人にも人気が高い。

New Yorkの街角から [1]

―― ニューヨークのタクシー ――

　通りを走る黄色いタクシー（yellow cab）は、マンハッタンの代表的な風景のひとつである。車の上にテレビ番組やブロードウェイのミュージカルの広告を掲げているタクシーもよく見かける。

　ジョン・F・ケネディ空港からマンハッタン市内までは、どのタクシーに乗っても均一料金（flat fare）で、チップを含めると約 65 ドル。地下鉄や空港バスを使う方が安く済むが、途中迷わずに行きたい時や荷物が沢山ある時は、楽で便利だ。

　タクシーに乗ったら、臆せずドライバーに話しかけてみるとよい。ニューヨークのタクシードライバーは、外国から来た人が多い。たいていの場合は、お国訛りのある英語で応えてくれる。

　出身国はさまざまだ。イギリスから来た男性は、動物園の飼育係だったそうだが、夢を求めてアメリカに移り住み、タクシードライバーをしながらお金を貯めている、と言う。また、別のドライバーはくじでグリーンカード（アメリカの永住権）が当たり、ウズベキスタンからニューヨークに移住してきたという。お金を貯めて年に 1 回は母国に帰り、親孝行しているそうだ。でも、「これ以外の職業に就くことはなかなか難しい」と言う。新天地での生活はバラ色、という訳にはいかないようだ。

　会話が進むと、お互いの英語に訛りがあるため、一度では通じないことがある。お互いに発音に気をつけながら何度か言い直して、やっと通じる、という時もある。「日本人は、r と l の発音が下手だよね」と言われると、「はい、その通り」と認めざるを得ない。「あなたの英語も訛りがあってよくわからないんだけどなぁ……」と心の中でつぶやきながら、おしゃべりに相槌を打つこともある。

　ドライバーの人生模様を垣間見ながら無事目的地に着いたなら、チップは気持ちよく、笑顔で渡そう。そうすればきっと、"Have a nice day!" と笑顔で送り出してくれるだろう。

UNIT 6 College Life

ニューヨークの学生生活

Rika's Report

Today let me report about my college life and some of the classes I am taking.

In my English class and other discussion-based classes, both teachers and students talk and hold discussions in a very relaxed manner. They even drink coffee during class. This is something that you would never see in Japanese universities.
5 Students are dressed very casually, too. It is common to see students walking around the campus in jeans and a T-shirt or a sweatshirt with the university's logo.

In writing class, Mr. Robbins, our teacher, sometimes talks about English grammar, but the funniest thing is that he often makes mistakes. The other day, he introduced a new sentence to us: "Starting in April, the new program will include a
10 variety of fieldwork." and explained that "Starting" is a gerund. I noticed he was wrong. I have studied English grammar since junior high school, so I could not stop myself from pointing out his mistake. "I think it's a present participle, isn't it?"

After an awkward pause, he replied, "Well, you're right. You know more about grammar than I do!" This sort of thing has happened several times. So now before
15 the class starts, my classmates always chuckle at me and say, "What's your question today, Rika?"

On the other hand, the class entitled Global Issues is fun and inspiring. Students have the chance to hold discussions via video conferencing with officials working at the United Nations or the American government. The topics, such as human rights, race and poverty, are diverse and applicable worldwide. It is so exciting to swap opinions face-to-face with a different official every time. It takes me a lot of time to prepare for this class, but joining in the discussions not only broadens my perspective but also connects me to various problems in the world.

I am so grateful that I was given the opportunity to study in New York by the university exchange program. Above all, New York is a great city where you can learn and experience things that you never could elsewhere in the world.

(349 words)

Notes

▶ **p. 30**

l. 10 **gerund**「動名詞」

l. 11 **could not stop myself from ...**「つい...したくなった」

l. 12 **present participle**「現在分詞」

l. 13 **after an awkward pause**「少し気まずい沈黙のあとで」

l. 15 **chuckle at ...**「...を笑ってからかう」

▶ **p. 31**

l. 1 **Global Issues**「国際問題」

l. 1 **inspiring**「刺激的な」

l. 2 **via video conferencing**「テレビ会議を通して」

l. 3 **the United Nations**「国際連合」 本部は 1st Ave. と East River に囲まれた E.42nd-48th St. にある。

l. 4 **applicable worldwide**「世界中に共通する」

l. 7 **connect me to ...**「...に私の関心を引き寄せてくれる」

国連のホームページでは、最新の国際情勢を知ることができる。Cyber School Bus という学生向けのサイトでは、平和・人権・貧困・人種などの諸問題について、専門家との Q & A 形式でわかりやすく学ぶことができる。

I Comprehension

次の各文が本文の内容と合っている場合は T、間違っている場合は F を選びなさい。

1. T / F   In English and discussion-based classes, teachers and students exchange opinions in a very relaxed manner.
2. T / F   The writing teacher is not good at explaining about grammar.
3. T / F   Rika doesn't like the class called Global Issues because it requires a lot of preparation at home.

II Useful Expressions

(   ) の中に適語を入れ、それぞれの和文に合う英文を作りなさい。

1. 彼のおかしなコスチュームを見て、思わず笑ってしまいました。
   I (   ) (   ) (   ) (   ) from laughing when I looked at his funny costume.

2. そのクラスでは多くの野外活動を行います。
   The class will (   ) many outside activities.

3. この大学で勉強できる機会に恵まれ、とってもうれしいです。
   I am so happy that I was (   ) (   ) (   ) (   ) study at this university.

III Listening

ダイアローグを聞き、空所を埋めなさい。

　　—Rika and her teacher talk about grammar in writing class.

　　Rika:　Mr. Robbins, I have a question. (   ) (   ) (   ) an indefinite article before "discount" when you say "I'd like to (   ) (   ) (   )"?

Mr. Robbins:　Oh, (   ) (   ). I forgot the article.

　　Rika:　Also, can you say "get discounts"?

Mr. Robbins:　No, you can't. "Get a discount" is a (   ) (   ).

　　Rika:　Thank you, Mr. Robbins.

Mr. Robbins:　Do you have any other questions, Rika?

　　Rika:　No more for today!

Unit 6

Activity

英語で自己紹介をするための原稿を書いてみましょう。

Hello everyone,

　My name is _____.

My nickname is _____, so please call me _____.

　I came from Japan. I'm a student at _____ University, majoring in _____.

The University is located in _____.

　I came to study here because _____
_____.

　In my free time, I like to _____
_____.

　If you have any questions about Japan, please feel free to ask me. I'd be happy to answer them.

Thank you!

UNIT 7

Food in New York

ニューヨーク 食探検

Rika's Report

These days, I often visit the East Village with my friends. It is an interesting place where you can hang out and find ethnic enclaves on different blocks. These areas have been inhabited by immigrants from India, Ukraine and South Korea, and are sometimes called by their nicknames, such as Little Ukraine or Koreatown. You can enjoy specialties that are typical to those countries.

When you walk for a few minutes from Astor Place to the east, you can find a lot of Japanese-style restaurants with their signs in Japanese. The food they serve ranges from *udon* noodles, *okonomiyaki*, *yakitori* and casual pub-style food to traditional dishes, such as *kaiseki* and *yuba* courses, which are served only by high-end restaurants in Tokyo. It is the best place to stop by when you are craving Japanese food. Panya Bakery sells Japanese *bento* boxes and sweets. I was thrilled to find *mamedaifuku* in this store. I just couldn't resist buying one!

Also, *ramen* noodles have become everyone's favorite in today's New York. Just recently, Angie and I stopped by Momofuku, one of those *ramen* restaurants that is getting attention. There we saw a lot of customers walking in and out. The customers had no trouble using chopsticks, which was amazing to me! I wanted to eat authentic Japanese *ramen*, but what they actually served was a bit expensive and unique. There was little soup over the noodles and the way the toppings were arranged was what I had never seen before. I think over the years that New York-style *ramen* has been modernized and changed to meet the more stylish tastes of New Yorkers.

Veselka is a traditional Ukrainian restaurant in the East Village that you should definitely try. The store is filled with modern art goods and colorful matryoshka dolls, and is often visited by artists, photographers, actors and actresses in the city. Simple Ukrainian dishes such as borscht, stuffed cabbage, and Ukrainian dumplings are reasonable and easy on your stomach. There are many regulars and some people come here just for the holiday pancake brunch.

Next time I visit the East Village, I would like to try Korean food which is now popular in Japan.

(364 words)

Notes

▶ p. 34
- *l. 1* **the East Village** 「イーストビレッジ」マンハッタンの東南地区。その多様な人種構成や民族文化が特徴である。
- *l. 2* **hang out** 「ぶらぶら歩く」
- *l. 2* **ethnic enclaves** 「少数民族の居住地」
- *l. 4* **Little Ukraine** 「リトル・ウクライナ」イーストビレッジにあるウクライナ人地区の通称。
- *l. 4* **Koreatown** 「コリアタウン」イーストビレッジにある韓国人地区の通称。
- *l. 6* **Astor Place** 「アスタープレイス」E.8th St./4th Ave. の交差点周辺地域をさし、同名の地下鉄駅がある。
- *l. 8* **pub-style** 「居酒屋風の」
- *l. 9* **high-end** 「高級な」
- *l. 11* **Panya** 「パンヤ」日本のパン、菓子、弁当などを売っているイーストビレッジの店。

▶ p. 35
- *l. 7* **matryoshka dolls** 「マトリョーシカ人形」ロシアの伝統的な民芸品。人形の中に人形が入っている「入れ子構造」が特徴。
- *l. 9* **borscht** 「ボルシチ」赤かぶを使ったロシアの家庭料理。
- *l. 9* **stuffed cabbage** 「ロールキャベツ」
- *l. 9* **Ukrainian dumplings** 「ウクライナ風の水餃子」
- *l. 10* **regulars** 「常連客たち」

TIPS

NY の街角では、各国料理をアレンジした惣菜を量り売りする Deli をよく見かける。栄養のバランスや量を選ぶことができて、チップの心配もなく気軽に利用できる eat-in タイプの Deli と、take-out だけの Deli がある。

I Comprehension

次の各文が本文の内容と合っている場合は T、間違っている場合は F を選びなさい。

1. T / F   The East Village has been inhabited by immigrants from India, Ukraine and South Korea.
2. T / F   You can eat a variety of Japanese food including those served only by high-end restaurants in Tokyo.
3. T / F   Rika thought the *ramen* in New York is tasty and reasonable.

II Useful Expressions

(   ) の中に適語を入れ、それぞれの和文に合う英文を作りなさい。

1. 原宿は、週末ぶらぶら歩くのに面白いところです。
   Harajuku is an interesting place where you can (   ) (   ) on weekends.

2. その店でデンマーク製のおもちゃを見つけ、すごくうれしかったです。
   I was (   ) (   ) find Danish toys at the store.

3. あまりに眠くて、うっかりソファで寝てしまいました。
   I was so drowsy that I couldn't (   ) (   ) on the sofa.

III Listening

ダイアローグを聞き、空所を埋めなさい。

—Rika visits Veselka in the East Village.

Rika: (   ) (   ) (   ) a menu?

Waiter: (*The waiter brings a menu.*) Here you are.

Rika: (   ) (   ) (   ) the borscht? How big is a bowl?

Waiter: Well, it's not so big. About this size. (*The waiter shows the size with his hands.*)

Rika: Are there any Ukrainian desserts?

Waiter: Sure. You can see a list of desserts (   ) (   ) (   ) of the menu.

Activity

下のメニューを見ながら次の文を作り、クラスで発表してみましょう。

I'll have (　　　　), (　　　　　) and (　　　　　) for breakfast.

I'll pay (　　　　　) dollars and (　　　　　) cents.

Breakfast Specials

Bread & Pancakes

Bagel w/ Butter	2.50
Bagel w/ Cream Cheese	3.00
French Toast	4.00
Pancakes	4.00
Pancakes w/ Choice of Platter	6.50

Beverages

Freshly Ground Coffee	3.00
Decaffeinated Coffee	3.00
Tea	3.00
Cappuccino	4.00
Hot Chocolate	4.50
Iced Coffee	3.50
Iced Tea	3.50
Fresh Orange Juice	3.50

Platter

Two Eggs Any Style	3.00
Bacon & Eggs	4.00
Ham & Eggs	4.00
Sausage & Eggs	4.00
Cheese Omelet	5.00
Ham & Cheese Omelet	5.50
Vegetarian Omelet	5.50

(All Served w/ Home Fried Potatoes & Toast)

UNIT 8
Skyscrapers are the Landmarks

高層ビルは道しるべ

Rika's Report

When walking in the city, I love to look up at the tall buildings. Their overwhelming heights and unique shapes always intrigue me.

One of them is the Empire State Building. Soaring 1,046 feet above midtown Manhattan, it has always been a symbol of New York City. Another one is the
5 Chrysler Building. Its Art Deco design and needle-sharp spire are very impressive. The Flatiron Building, which looks exactly like a "flat iron," appears in the movie, *Spiderman*. These buildings are all popular with photo-taking tourists.

Such skyscrapers are a part of my life in the city because they are my landmarks. When I get lost in Soho and see the Empire State Building ahead, it
10 means I am facing north. A building can also tell you where you are if you get out of the wrong subway exit.

Today in the late afternoon, Angie came along with me to visit the Empire State Building, since neither of us had ever gone up to the top. We walked out of the elevator on the 86th floor onto an observation deck, and what we saw there was
15 just incredible.

The deck was facing towards the sunset where the reflections of the crowds of skyscrapers on Wall Street were glittering silver and orange in the sunlight. We did not leave there until the silhouettes of the buildings melted into darkness and were replaced by beautiful illuminations. The scene reminded us of the movie, *Sleepless in Seattle*. For those who are not familiar with the movie, let me highlight its climax.

—The heroine is looking at the red heart-shaped illumination on the Empire State Building from the top-floor restaurant of Rockefeller Center with her fiancé. But she suddenly decides that she should meet the love of her life, leaving her fiancé behind. She hurries to the observatory of the Empire State Building, only to find it empty. She remains standing there, disappointed, when suddenly the man and his son come back to get the bag which the son had left behind, and they finally meet. —

Both Angie and I were recalling that scene and feeling a bit romantic. I guess Angie wished it was Jonathan, not me, who was with her tonight! (369 words)

Notes

▶ p. 38
- *l. 2* **intrigue**「興味を引く」
- *l. 3* **Empire State Building**「エンパイア・ステート・ビル」1931 年に完成した、34th St./5th Ave. に NY のシンボルとしてそびえ立つ 102 階建てのビル。
- *l. 5* **Chrysler Building**「クライスラー・ビル」E.42nd St. グランドセントラル駅のすぐ近くのビル。
- *l. 5* **Art Deco**「アール・デコ」1910 年半ばから 1930 年代にかけてヨーロッパや NY で流行った装飾の様式。
- *l. 6* **Flatiron Building**「フラットアイアン・ビル」 1902 年に建てられた NY でもっとも古い高層ビルのひとつ。三角形の珍しい形で有名。
- *l. 9* **Soho**「ソーホー」グリニッチ・ビレッジの南に隣接する地域。

▶ p. 39
- *l. 1* **Wall Street**「ウォール街」ニューヨーク証券取引所がある世界の金融の中心地。
- *l. 3* **replaced by ...**「...にとって代わられた」
- *l. 3* **reminded us of ...**「私たちに ... を思い出させた」
- *l. 4* **highlight**「(ある部分を) 特に取り上げる」

Tips

映画 *Sleepless in Seattle*「めぐり逢えたら」は、妻を病気で失った男性と、その男性の声をラジオで聴いて心惹かれた雑誌記者の女性の恋を描いた物語。最後にエンパイア・ステート・ビルで運命の出会いをする。

I Comprehension

次の各文が本文の内容と合っている場合は **T**、間違っている場合は **F** を選びなさい。

1. T / F　The Chrysler Building is distinctive in its Art Deco design.
2. T / F　Soho is located to the north of the Empire State Building.
3. T / F　The Empire State Building plays an important role in the movie which both Rika and Angie remembered.

II Useful Expressions

（　）の中に適語を入れ、それぞれの和文に合う英文を作りなさい。

1. その部屋は北東に面しているので、暗くて寒い。
   The room is dark and cold, as it is (　　　　) (　　　　).

2. 古い商店街は新しいスーパーマーケットに入れ替わった。
   Old shopping malls (　　　) (　　　　) (　　　) new supermarkets.

3. 私が遅れて駅に着いた時は、すでに友人は去った後だった。
   I arrived at the station late, (　　　) (　) (　　　) my friend had already left.

III Listening

ダイアローグを聞き、空所を埋めなさい。

—Rika and Angie are at the observatory of the Empire State Building.

Rika: Wow, it's gorgeous! We can (　　　) (　　　) (　　) the whole city from here.

Angie: Yeah, I think it's so amazing that all of New York looks like a miniature city.

Rika: Is that the Chrysler Building over there?

Angie: Right. The Empire and the Chrysler (　　　) (　　　). One night, I (　　　　) the Chrysler (　　　) the Empire and got lost.

Rika: We should (　　　) (　　　) (　　　) directions at night, shouldn't we?

Activity

本文に書かれた NY のビルの特徴と下のイラストを参考にして、次の a～d の建物がマンハッタンのどこにあるか、(　) に記号を書き入れてみましょう。

(a) Empire State Building　　(b) Chrysler Building

(c) Rockefeller Center　　(d) Citigroup Center

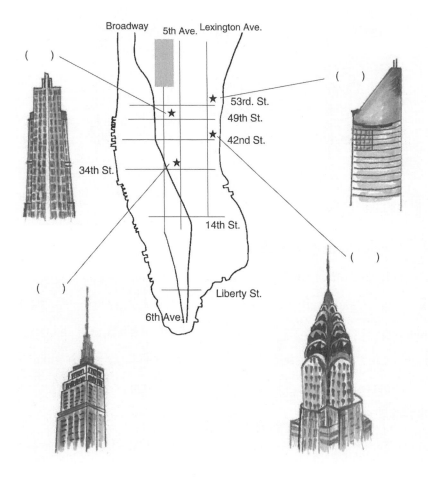

UNIT 9 Dazzling Brooklyn

活気づくブルックリン

Rika's Report

A friend of mine, who has lived in New York for a long time, said, "You must see the new Brooklyn because it's so exciting." So I took the subway running under the East River and arrived at Williamsburg in the Brooklyn District.

Twelve years ago, the town had a rather dreary look. There were only run-down brick factories and their ruins. Even in the daytime, people felt it a bit scary to walk down the streets. Now the town has transformed itself into an open, relaxed, and fashionable area. Williamsburg and Yokohama are very much alike. Both are located on waterfronts dotted with many stylish stores inside renovated old warehouses.

My friend recommended that I check out Beacon's Closet, a second-hand vintage clothes store, and also Wythe Hotel. They are both in refurbished brick factories and are getting a lot of attention nowadays. You can find a variety of vintage clothes and bags, accessories, and bric-a-brac displayed in Beacon's Closet. If you choose an outfit from this store, it will make you look more stylish than if you were to buy clothes from a chain store in downtown Manhattan.

There was a long line up in front of Wythe Hotel. I asked a doorman what was happening. He said to me, "There is a popular bar on the top floor. It has a spectacular view of Manhattan beyond the East River, but it's extremely crowded on the weekends." Then, he winked at me and continued, "If you stay in New York for another week, you should come back here after 5 p.m. on a Monday afternoon."

5   So I settled for some cranberry juice in a less crammed bar on the first floor, and walked to a park near the East River. Then I realized why people wanted to go to the top floor of Wythe Hotel so much. Manhattan stretching beyond the river was just gorgeous—especially in the early evening when the sun reflects on the buildings, making them glitter beautifully.

10 Sometime I would like to go back to the park with my friends to make a toast to the amazing view of Manhattan.

(356 words)

Notes

▶ p. 42
- *l. 3* **Williamsburg**「ウィリアムズバーグ」ブルックリン区の地下鉄 Bedford Avenue 駅を中心とする地域。マンハッタンから移住した若い世代が多く住む。
- *l. 4* **dreary look**「殺風景な様子」
- *l. 4* **run-down**「荒廃した」
- *l. 8* **dotted with ...**「... が点在する」
- *l. 10* **Beacon's Closet**「ビーコンズ・クローゼット」ウィリアムズバーグにある人気の古着店。服やアクセサリーからレトロなインテリア小物まで品揃えが豊富である。
- *l. 11* **Wythe Hotel**「ワイス・ホテル」ウィリアムズバーグにある、お洒落な若者たちの間で人気のホテル。
- *l. 13* **bric-a-brac**「古い小物」

▶ p. 43
- *l. 5* **settle for ...**「とりあえず ... でしのぐ」
- *l. 10* **make a toast to ...**「... に乾杯する」

Tips

Brooklyn 地区では、マンハッタンから歩いて渡れる Brooklyn Bridge や、マンハッタン南部を一望できる Brooklyn Heights Promenade も人気の場所。ここから見るマンハッタンの夜景は、NY の代表的な風景として雑誌や広告によく使われている。

I Comprehension

次の各文が本文の内容と合っている場合は T、間違っている場合は F を選びなさい。

1. T / F   Williamsburg and Yokohama are alike because both of them are located on waterfronts.
2. T / F   You should visit the bar at the top of Wythe Hotel before 5 p.m. on a Monday since it gets crowded after that time.
3. T / F   Rika had a glass of wine in a less crammed bar at the same hotel.

II Useful Expressions

(　) の中に適語を入れ、それぞれの和文に合う英文を作りなさい。

1. その通りは、高級でおしゃれな店が点在しています。
   The street (　　) (　　　　　) with posh and stylish stores.

2. 最近、外国人観光客の間で、富士山登山が人気です。
   Climbing Mt. Fuji is (　　　　　) a lot of (　　　　　) from foreign visitors these days.

3. その店にはステーキはなく、結局ハンバーグを食べることにしました。
   They had no steak at the restaurant, so we (　　　　　) (　　　　) a hamburger.

III Listening

ダイアローグを聞き、空所を埋めなさい。

　　—Rika talks to a clerk at Beacon's Closet.

Rika: (　　　) (　　　　) are these vintage jeans?
Clerk: Seven hundred dollars.
Rika: How old are they?
Clerk: They are probably (　　　) (　　　) (　　　) (　　　).
Rika: If I buy them together with that blouse over there, do I get a discount?
Clerk: I'm afraid not. They are (　　　) (　　　) (　　　) (　　　).

Activity

次の **Brooklyn Bridge** のツアー案内を見て、下の問題に答えましょう。

Brooklyn Bridge Walk on Weekends
Join a fun and scenic walk from Manhattan to Brooklyn!

Days:	Saturdays and Sundays
Time:	10:30 a.m. to 11:30 a.m. Please make sure to meet with us 15 minutes before the tour starts.
Departure:	The main entrance of the Manhattan Municipal Building
Points of Interest:	Halfway across the bridge is a great spot to take photos and observe all the activities on and over the East River. After exiting the Bridge in Brooklyn, you can enjoy lunch and a magnificent view at one of the nearby restaurants.
Tips:	Bring water, especially on a hot day.
Contact:	info@newyorkwalker.com

FREE but Reservations Required

Questions

1. At what time do the participants meet?
2. From which side of the bridge does the tour start, Manhattan or Brooklyn?
3. How much does the tour cost?
4. What is advisable for walking on a hot day?
5. Are reservations necessary?

UNIT 10
Email from the Teacher (1)

ニューヨークへのメッセージ（1）

Hi Rika,

Thank you for updating me on your recent experiences in New York. Your reports on the streets and avenues, subways and skyscrapers have reminded me of a lot of the things I experienced when I visited
5   New York thirteen years ago. Every time I receive a report from you, my memories come flooding back and I'm filled with the same excitement and happiness that I felt at that time.
First, I was amazed by the drastic changes Brooklyn has undergone these past years! I was also curious about the food you reported on.
10 Back then there were only a few authentic Japanese food stores and restaurants, and they were very expensive. It's so great that you can now easily enjoy a variety of Japanese foods such as *yakitori, takoyaki* and *daifuku* at reasonable prices.
As you know, sweets that are favored in New York always become
15 popular in Tokyo. Until some time ago, doughnuts were a hit among young people—represented by the famous Krispy Kreme. But now pancakes are taking over. There is always a long line of people waiting

in front of the recently opened Sarabeth's Shinagawa. Of course, I'd like to try some of Veselka's pancakes someday.

The classes you described are very unique in the ways they are conducted. Due to the small number of students in your English classes, you have many more opportunities to communicate with your fellow students and the teacher than if you were in a larger class.

Also, video conferencing with UN or government officials—whom you normally would never be able to meet in person—sounds like a big undertaking. It's a nice hands-on experience for you and other students who are interested in international relations.

I'm also happy that you have brushed up on your English. You know that learning the basics and continually making an effort are so important. Otherwise, your English won't improve even though you are living in an English-speaking country. Rika, you are a good model for other students.

Well, take care of yourself and enjoy the rest of your stay. Get the most out of your experiences in New York, a city full of diversity!

Best,
May J. Sato

(368 words)

Notes

▶ **p. 46**
- *l. 5* **memories come flooding back**「思い出が蘇り押し寄せる」
- *l. 8* **curious about ...**「... を興味深く思う」
- *l. 16* **Krispy Kreme**「クリスピー・クリーム」アメリカのドーナツチェーン店。ニューヨークで人気が出たのち、世界中に店舗が広がった。

▶ **p. 47**
- *l. 1* **Sarabeth's**「サラベス」アッパーウェストサイドにある朝食とブランチの有名店。特にパンケーキとフレンチトーストが人気。
- *l. 2* **Veselka**「ベセルカ」イーストビレッジにあるウクライナ料理店（Unit 7 参照）
- *l. 4* **due to ...**「... という理由で」
- *l. 7* **UN** The United Nations の略称。（Unit 6 参照）
- *l. 8* **in person**「直接」
- *l. 8* **big undertaking**「壮大な企画」
- *l. 9* **hands-on experience**「実際に体験すること」
- *l. 16* **get the most out of ...**「... を最大限に生かす」

Eメールの書き方 ❶

Rika が渡航前に、留学先大学の生活担当アドバイザー Miller さんに質問したメールです。メールの基本的な書き方や質問の仕方を学びましょう。

Subject（件名）は相手がひと目で用件を理解できるように短く簡潔に書く。

初めてメールする相手、目上の人、ビジネスメールなどでは、敬称の Dear を用いる。(Dear Mr. Robbins,/ Dear John,)
ただし、友だちや親しい人には Hi ＋ファーストネームでもよい。(Hi Angie,)

Subject: Inquiries about dorm life

Dear Ms. Miller,

Thank you for sending me the handbook for international students. I found a lot of useful information in it. Since you kindly told me that I can ask any question related to housing, clothes and things to bring, etc, I would like to ask you the following questions.

1) What is the weather like there in early April? Do I need a warm coat?
2) I will take my PC with me. Does every room in the dorm have wi-fi?
3) Do you have a shared kitchen? Can I bring an electric rice cooker?

I am leaving for New York on Friday, March 20, which is two weeks from now.
I am very excited and looking forward to meeting everybody then.

Best wishes,
Rika Tanaka

目的はメールの始めの方に書くと、相手に理解されやすい。

質問は必ずしも箇条書きでなくてもよいが、具体的に簡潔に書こう。

結句としてよく使う。親しい相手には、Best, とだけ書くこともある。

NOTES

Thank you for ...ing「...してくれたことに対し感謝する」返礼として文頭に来る定型句。
I would like to ...「...がしたい」の丁寧な言い方
the following ...「次の／下記の」
shared kitchen「共同の台所」
two weeks from now「今から数えて2週間後」
look forward to ...「...することを楽しみにしている」to のあとは名詞または動名詞が来るので注意。

Unit 10

Activity　Eメールを書いてみましょう❶

インターネットで海外の大学が掲載している留学生用ハンドブックを見つけ、わからないことを質問するメールを書いてみましょう。

```
Subject: _____

_____
_____
_____
_____
_____
_____
_____
_____
_____
_____
_____
```

関連表現

- 何かについて質問をする

    I would like to know when the application deadline is.（願書の締め切りはいつですか？）

    Could you tell me when the orientation starts?（オリエンテーションはいつ始まりますか？）

    Please let me know if there is a refrigerator in the room.（部屋に冷蔵庫があるかどうか教えてください）

- 相手のメールや行為に対し、礼を言う

    Thank you for your email.（メールをありがとうございました）

    Thank you for your prompt reply.（さっそくのお返事をありがとうございました）

- 文末の表現として

    I look forward to hearing from you soon.（ご連絡をお待ちしています）

    I hope you have a great weekend.（よい週末をお過ごしください）

メール作成上の注意点

◎ 全体に文章は短く簡潔に書く。

◎ 2〜3行ごとにスペースをとり間隔を空けると相手は読みやすい。

◎ 質問は短く具体的に書く。回りくどくならないように気をつけよう。

A Japanese in New York [2]

Kenichiro Sano
—Student at the State University of New York Stony Brook

佐野さんは東京外国語大学の4年生です。NY州立大学ストーニーブルック校に交換留学生としてやってきました。現在、統計学やビジネスの授業などをとっています。ディスカッションを中心とするクラスではさまざまな国から来た留学生が意見を活発に交わし、とても刺激的です。授業のない日はソーホーやノリータへ行ったり、趣味のスタンドアップ・コメディを練習したり、思い切りNY生活を楽しんでいます。文化や言葉の壁にぶつかったときは、決して諦めないという強い気持ちで臨むことが大切だと感じています。

英語のナレーションを聞き、1〜5のアンダーラインの箇所に当てはまるものをa〜cの中から選びなさい。

1. He is studying statistics and _____ at the State University of New York.
   a. literature   b. business   c. mathematics

2. In the discussion-based classes, some students are from Asia including _____.
   a. Nepal   b. India   c. Indonesia

3. On weekends, he goes to Soho or Nolita to enjoy looking at _____.
   a. galleries   b. musicals   c. bars and cafes

4. When you can't get your message across, the most important thing is to _____.
   a. never give up   b. apologize quickly   c. ask for someone's help

5. He found what he learned at his Japanese university has been quite _____ what he is learning now.
   a. different from   b. harder than   c. useful for

Notes

Nolita ノリータ (North of Little Italy)。リトルイタリーの北側に位置し、ソーホーと同じく若者に人気のあるカフェやお洒落なブティックなどが立ち並ぶ。
stand-up comedy 政治・文化・人種などをネタにひとりで行うコメディ・パフォーマンス。
get one's message across 考えなどを相手に伝え、わからせる。

New Yorkの街角から [2]

—— パブリック・アート ——

　ニューヨークでアートを楽しめる場所は、美術館やギャラリーだけではない。街を歩くと、ユニークな形のオブジェや動物のフィギュア、目を引くウォール・ペインティング……あちこちでアートに出会うことができる。

　イーストビレッジの入り口にもなっているアスタープレイスの交差点には、The Cubeと呼ばれる巨大な立方体のオブジェがある。このオブジェは、かなりの力が必要だが、回転させることができる。その時によって立方体の見え方が変わるのが面白い。

　金融地区のウォール街には、Charging Bull（突進する雄牛）と呼ばれる巨大な牛のブロンズ像がある。この雄牛は、1989年にイタリア人の彫刻家によって無許可のままニューヨーク証券取引所のすぐ近くに設置され、のちに2ブロックほど離れた現在の場所に移動されたそうだ。Bullは、「商売繁盛」「上昇相場」を体現していると言われ、その通り、四本の足に力を溜めて猛進しそうな姿勢を取っている。ここを訪れる多くの観光客がこのブロンズ像と一緒に記念写真を撮り、雄牛の体や頭をなでている。

　レンガ造りの古い建物や塀に施されたアートと広告を兼ねたペインティングは、ネオンサインや電光掲示板とはまた違う、少しレトロな雰囲気をかもしだす表現として、ニューヨークの街の風景に溶け込んでいる。ブルックリンには、レンガ造りの工場や倉庫だった建物を改造してできたお洒落なショップやレストラン、ホテルが沢山あり、人気を集めている。大きなレンガの壁には、紙のポスターを貼る代わりに、直接広告やイベントのスケジュール表が描かれていたりする。

　このように、ニューヨークのパブリック・アートは、誰でも近づいて触れることができる身近な存在である。他にも期間限定で、公園や街角など屋外や、駅、オフィスビルなどの屋内で、誰でも楽しめる展示やイベントがよく開催される。思いがけない発見を期待しながら、いろいろなエリアを歩いてみよう。

UNIT 11 Friends from Different Countries

異文化コミュニケーションを楽しむ

Rika's Report

It has been five months since I came to study in New York. There are many international students from different countries living in my university dorm. They are from such countries as Korea, Taiwan, Hong Kong, Brazil, Germany, and France.

In the beginning, I could not understand what they were saying—because some of them talked like a bullet train and others spoke with peculiar accents. I also did not know how to approach them to become friends. But now I have a great time with them. Let me tell you how I have successfully made a lot of friends since coming to New York.

An important key to making friends with people from different countries is respecting their language and culture, and becoming interested in even a tiny thing related to their homeland. For instance, I memorized "Hello!" in each of their languages—*Annyeonhaseyo, Nihao, Hola, Guten Tag, Bonjour* and such. By doing so, a good atmosphere develops and dialogues can begin. They will in turn start asking questions about your country.

Also, food can be a catalyst for creating friendship across national borders. The other day, my friends took me to a Japanese restaurant to celebrate my 21st birthday. An item on the menu quickly caught my eye. It said *Hibachi* in Japanese. Can you guess what it is? The Japanese chef cooked rice, shrimp and vegetables on a steaming grill, sometimes throwing them high up in the air to mix them—it looked like a magic show. That night, my friends kept asking a lot of questions about Japanese food and culture. It became an unforgettable birthday for me.

 I wonder if you have ever heard of Beer Pong? It is a game I often play at the dorm with my friends. You place ten paper cups filled with beer or water on both edges of a long table. Then players standing on both sides throw ping pong balls into the cups from across the table. The game is very fun and relaxing. It helps you to get acquainted with someone you have first met, even if you are shy or do not speak English well.

(358 words)

Notes

▶ **p. 52**
- *l. 2* **university dorm**「学生寮」
- *l. 6* **bullet train**「新幹線」
- *l. 14* **in turn**「交代で」
- *l. 16* **catalyst for ...**「...を促すもの」

▶ **p. 53**
- *l. 2* **Hibachi**「ヒバチ」日本料理の鉄板焼きを指す。
- *l. 4* **steaming grill**「熱い鉄板」
- *l. 7* **Beer Pong**「ビアポン」飲物を入れたコップと卓球の球を使って行うゲーム。(やり方は本文参照)
- *l. 11* **get acquainted with ...**「...と知り合いになる」

TIPS

「ビアポン」はパーティーゲームとしてだけでなく、スポーツとしても世界各国で競技されている。公式ルールはBPONG.COMが制定しており、毎年1月にラスベガスでワールドシリーズ大会が開催される。

I Comprehension

次の各文が本文の内容と合っている場合は **T**、間違っている場合は **F** を選びなさい。

1. T / F   Rika understood her friends' English well since they tried to speak slowly for her.

2. T / F   The key to making friends with students from overseas is to have respect for and an interest in their language and culture.

3. T / F   In Beer Pong, you throw ping pong balls into empty paper cups.

II Useful Expressions

(　) の中に適語を入れ、それぞれの和文に合う英文を作りなさい。

1. スポンジケーキをうまく焼くコツは、最初に卵の白身をよく泡立てることです。
   The (　　) (　　) baking a good sponge cake is to beat the egg whites well first.

2. その店の黄色い看板が目を引きました。
   The yellow signboard at the store (　　　　) (　　　) (　　　　).

3. 私の町に住む、なるべく多くの外国人と親しくなりたいです。
   I want to (　　　) (　　　　　　) (　　　　) many of the foreigners living in my town.

III Listening

ダイアローグを聞き、空所を埋めなさい。

　—Rika talks with her friend at a Japanese restaurant.

Friend: What does *Hibachi* (　　　) (　　　　) in Japanese?

Rika: Actually, it's a heating device used in the old days.

Friend: I saw it in a Samurai movie. It's not (　　　　) (　　　　　) (　　　) heat up the entire house, is it?

Rika: You're right. It's no longer used in Japanese houses today. But some foreigners like to use it (　　　) (　　　) (　　　　　) in their houses.

Friend: I see.

Unit 11

Activity

次の英文を読んで、日本のどんなことについて書いてあるか、あててみましょう。

(1) It is Japan's highest mountain and a symbol of Japan.
　　　　　　　　　　　　　　　　　_____

(2) It is the super-express train and called "The Bullet Train."
　　　　　　　　　　　　　　　　　_____

(3) It is the tea ceremony where powdered green tea is served.
　　　　　　　　　　　　　　　　　_____

(4) It is called "beef bowl." It is one of the most popular fast foods in Japan.
　　　　　　　　　　　　　　　　　_____

(5) It is a Japanese-style pancake made with meat, seafood, eggs, and chopped cabbage.
　　　　　　　　　　　　　　　　　_____

(6) It is the traditional Japanese art of arranging flowers.
　　　　　　　　　　　　　　　　　_____

(7) It is the "rock-scissors-paper" game played between two or more people when they want to make a decision.
　　　　　　　　　　　　　　　　　_____

(8) It is a written fortune which can be bought at shrines and temples.
　　　　　　　　　　　　　　　　　_____

(9) It is "cherry blossom viewing." In the spring, people enjoy viewing cherry blossoms in full bloom.
　　　　　　　　　　　　　　　　　_____

(10) It is a light cotton kimono worn at summer events like fireworks displays. It is also used as sleeping wear.
　　　　　　　　　　　　　　　　　_____

Unit 11　Friends from Different Countries　▪ 55

UNIT 12 Musicals on a Shoestring

安くミュージカルを見る方法

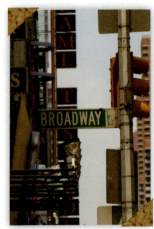

Rika's Report

There are a number of ways to see Broadway shows cheaply in New York. I have used some of these ways to see a few nice musicals on my shoestring budget.

Wicked—which I just saw last weekend—is a story about two young girls who later appear as the Good Witch of the North and the Wicked Witch of the West in *The Wizard of Oz*. Since this piece is full of songs and dances, you can enjoy it even if you do not understand English well.

To see this musical, I reserved a ticket through the Internet just one day before the show. The seat was in the fourth row near the stage and the price was forty dollars cheaper than a regular ticket. Do you want to know why I could get such a good seat at a reasonable price? There is a secret to this. It was one of the Partial View Seats, which are so close to the stage wings that you can't see part of the stage from the angle where you are seated. But it didn't bother me at all. I rather enjoyed the feverish dancing and dynamic actions being performed so close to me.

I also liked one line spoken by the green-faced Elphaba, "I'm feeling wicked for the first time," when she met the man who was her first love. Isn't this line fantastic?

Furthermore, if you like more avant-garde or eccentric musicals known as Off-Broadway shows, I recommend seeing one by the Blue Man Group. Three men, all in blue except for their eyes, do the funniest and strangest acts you could ever imagine, without saying a word. Astor Place Theatre is a small theater with less than three hundred seats and is always full. But there is also a secret way for college students to get a cheap ticket for this show. You go to the theater one hour before the show and present your student ID at the window. If there are some tickets left, you can get a Student Rush Ticket for thirty-two dollars. Isn't it a real bargain?

　Well, Broadway shows are really fun. Besides that, you might come across some celebrities at the theater. I would faint if I found Johnny Depp sitting next to me!

(381 words)

Notes

▶ **p. 56**

- *l. 2* **on a shoestring**「節約して」
- *l. 3* ***Wicked***「ウィキッド」「オズの魔法使い」をもとにしたミュージカル。「良い北の魔女」(Good Witch of the North) グリンダと「悪い西の魔女」(Wicked Witch of the West) エルファバの友情を描いている。
- *l. 5* ***The Wizard of Oz***「オズの魔法使い」ライマン・フランク・ボームの1900年作の童話。
- *l.10* **Partial View Seats**「部分的に舞台がさえぎられて見えない席」
- *l. 14* **green-faced Elphaba**「緑色の顔のエルファバ」エルファバは生まれた時から皮膚が緑色である。
- *l. 14* **"I'm feeling wicked for the first time."**「生まれて初めて幸せを感じる」

▶ **p. 57**

- *l. 1* **avant-garde**「前衛的な」
- *l. 2* **the Blue Man Group**「ブルーマン・グループ」全身を青色に塗った3人の男たちが無言で独自のパフォーマンスを披露する
- *l. 8* **Student Rush Ticket**「スチューデント・ラッシュ・チケット」学生証を見せるとチケットが通常より安くなる。

Tips

一般的にミュージカルを安く見るには、タイムズスクエアのTKTSに行くとよい。長蛇の列ができているが、かなりの確率で当日券が半額で手に入る。

I Comprehension

次の各文が本文の内容と合っている場合は T、間違っている場合は F を選びなさい。

1. T / F   Rika reserved a ticket for *Wicked* a day before the performance.
2. T / F   You can see the entire stage from a Partial View Seat.
3. T / F   Student Rush Tickets are more expensive than regular tickets.

II Useful Expressions

(　　) の中に適語を入れ、それぞれの和文に合う英文を作りなさい。

1. ホテルの部屋に窓がないことが少し気になった。
   The hotel room has no window, which (　　　　　) (　　　) a little.

2. きっと、想像もできないようなすごい体験ができると思いますよ。
   You will have the most exciting experience you (　　　) (　　　)
   (　　　　).

3. 近くのスーパーで、よく友達に出くわします。
   I often (　　　) (　　　) a friend of mine at a supermarket nearby.

III Listening

ダイアローグを聞き、空所を埋めなさい。

—Rika is at the box office at the theater.

Rika: I'd like a ticket for the Blue Man Show, please.
Woman: Do you want a Student Rush Ticket? It's (　　　) (　　　) (　　　) of a regular seat.
Rika: Can I (　　　) (　　　) (　　　) of the performers from the back?
Woman: Yes. The theater is very small.
Rika: Could you tell me (　　　) the show (　　　)?
Woman: It (　　　) (　　　) 10:00 p.m.
Rika: Thanks.

Activity

次の表は、Rika のお気に入り Broadway Musical の5本です。Musical のタイトルから推測して、それぞれの空欄に入るコメントを下の (a) ～ (d) より選んで入れてみましょう。

my favorite musicals...

	Musical	Theater	Comments
1	Wicked	Gershwin Theatre	The story of how two unlikely friends become the Wicked Witch and the Good Witch. It gives us a different perspective on the movie The Wizard of Oz.
2	Les Misérables	Imperial Theatre	
3	Chicago	Ambassador Theatre	
4	The Lion King	Minskoff Theatre	
5	Cinderella	Broadway Theatre	

(a) An exciting tale of greed, murder and show business. You can feel the fever of the actors and actresses through their thrilling performances.

(b) The pumpkin, the glass slipper, the masked ball and more…you'll love every romantic moment.

(c) You'll be impressed by broken dreams, passion, redemption, and survival of the human spirit against the background of a nation's revolution.

(d) Giraffes, birds, and many other animals celebrate together in this spectacular stage show with unforgettable music and breathtaking effects.

UNIT 13 Viva Grand Central Terminal!

100年の時を超えて

Rika's Report

　　Last week in my writing class, my assignment was to write an essay on the theme of "An introduction to a historic building in New York."

　　I decided to write about Grand Central Terminal which celebrated its centennial in 2013, one year before Tokyo Station. The Terminal is always crowded with commuters and tourists. Today, I came to do an audio tour around the Terminal. The audio guide not only guides you around, but it also gives you a detailed history and insight into this legendary station.

　　Since its opening in 1913, the Terminal has long served as a core of the public transportation services in and out of the city. In the early 20th century, the station was such a lively place, being used as a stage for various movies and dramas. There was a television station within the Terminal where live programs were aired. From the 1960s through the 1970s, due to severe financial conditions, there was a strong appeal from members of the railroad company and outside developers to dismantle the deteriorated building and replace it with a brand new skyscraper.

　　But, in contrast to another legendary station, Penn Station, which was demolished in 1963, New Yorkers took a stand to protect the Terminal from demolition. In 1990, the city finally decided to preserve the complex and renovate the interior and exterior of the old building.

 Now in the main concourse you can see shiny marble walls, fancy chandeliers, and a beautiful blue dome-shaped ceiling with a map of the constellations. The Terminal retains its original form and elaborately crafted details, thereby attracting many tourists from all over the world. There are also many restaurants, cafes, bakeries and souvenir shops within the station.

 When I finished the tour, I felt so hungry that I walked into the Oyster Bar, a famous seafood restaurant located on the ground floor. What I picked from among the various items on the menu was the Manhattan clam chowder. The waiter at the restaurant proudly said to me, "This restaurant is as old as the Terminal." When it gets a bit colder, I'm sure I will come back to this bar to eat plenty of fresh oysters.

(365 words)

Notes

▶ **p. 60**

- *l. 3* **Grand Central Terminal**「グランドセントラル駅」E.42nd St. にあるニューヨークの交通の拠点。観光名所としても有名。
- *l. 5* **audio tour**「携帯用音声ガイドを利用した見学」
- *l. 7* **insight into ...**「... を深く知ること」
- *l. 10* **various movies and dramas** 映画『北北西に進路を取れ』(1959 年) をはじめ、最近では人気ドラマ『ゴシップガール』のロケ地として度々使われている
- *l. 11* **television station within the Terminal**「駅構内のテレビ放送局」1950 年代には構内に CBS のスタジオがあり、生放送が行われていた
- *l. 15* **Penn Station** (Unit 1 参照)
- *l. 16* **take a stand**「断固とした立場をとる」

▶ **p. 61**

- *l. 4* **map of the constellations**「星座図」
- *l. 5* **elaborately crafted details**「精巧に施された装飾」
- *l. 10* **Manhattan clam chowder**「マンハッタン・クラムチャウダー」クラムチャウダーは、貝と野菜を使って作るスープ。乳白色のクリーム仕立てのニューイングランド風とは異なり、マンハッタン風はトマトベースで赤い色をしている。

Tips

グランドセントラル駅構内にある Oyster Bar は、新鮮な牡蠣・海老・カニ・ホタテ・鮭などの豊富なシーフード料理で人気のレストラン。冬期には、毎日 20 種類以上の生牡蠣がメニューに載る。迷ったら、店員にどの牡蠣がお薦めかを聞けば親切に教えてくれる。

I Comprehension

次の各文が本文の内容と合っている場合は T、間違っている場合は F を選びなさい。

1. T / F　Grand Central Terminal celebrated its centennial one year after Tokyo Station.
2. T / F　There was a radio station within the Terminal.
3. T / F　The famous Oyster Bar opened when the Terminal was constructed.

II Useful Expressions

（　）の中に適語を入れ、それぞれの和文に合う英文を作りなさい。

1. 新宿駅は、東京の郊外に住む人々にとって中心的役割を担っています。
   Shinjuku Station (　　　) (　　　) a core station for those who live in the suburbs of Tokyo.

2. ひどい雨のため、旅行は中止となった。
   The tour was cancelled (　　　) (　　　) heavy rain.

3. あまりにお腹が空いたので、駅弁を買い、車中でたいらげた。
   I was (　　　) hungry (　　　) I bought a lunchbox at the station and ate it all on the train.

III Listening

ダイアローグを聞き、空所を埋めなさい。

—Rika eats at the Oyster Bar.

Waiter: What (　　　) (　　　) (　　　)?
　Rika: I'd like the Manhattan clam chowder. Does it (　　　) (　　　) bread?
Waiter: Yes, but you can have crackers, too.
　Rika: (*Pointing at an item on the menu*) Do these oysters come from Japan?
Waiter: They are from *Kumamoto*. Do you want some?
　Rika: Yes, I'd like to (　　　) (　　　) (　　　) (　　　).

Activity

次の Grand Central Terminal のツアー案内を見て、問題に答えましょう。

Audio Tour

MTA Metro-North Railroad, which operates the Terminal, has teamed up with Orpheo USA, one of the world's most experienced producers of audio tours, to give tourists, travelers and locals alike a history of the terminal filled with interesting details and insights.

Orpheo's state-of-the-art audio device and headset comes with a free map of the terminal for just $8 for adults, with discounts for seniors and the disabled at $7, and students and children at $6.

THE AUDIO TOUR IS AVAILABLE SEVEN DAYS A WEEK (CLOSED ONLY ON THANKSGIVING DAY AND CHIRISTMAS DAY) AT SPECIALLY-MARKED "GCT TOUR" WINDOWS ON THE MAIN CONCOURSE. HOURS ARE 9 A.M. TO 6 P.M., BUT MAY BE EXTENDED DURING THE HOLIDAYS.

The tour is available in English, French, Spanish, Japanese, Italian, and German.

(www.grandcentralterminal.com/info/tours より抜粋)

Questions

1. What equipment do the participants of the audio tour rent?
2. What can the participants of the audio tour learn?
3. How much is the cost of the audio tour for students?
4. When is the audio tour not available?
5. Where do visitors pay for the audio tour?

UNIT 14 Markets are Fun

マーケットは最高！

Rika's Report

Today I will talk about markets where you can have fun as well as get the best deals on unique vintage and antique items.

Markets are held in many parts of Manhattan on weekends. One of my favorites is the flea market held in a large parking lot in the East Village. I become so fascinated rummaging through things in the stalls or just browsing that I forget about the time. You can get everything here—vintage clothes, books, accessories, expensive silverware and antique furniture at fairly reasonable prices.

Last weekend, I was there with Angie. My first buy was an old coffee tin can which cost me five dollars. Angie said, "If I were you I would've bargained more, but I love the color." It must have been vivid red and blue when it was new, but now the color is faded and smoky. Angie has decorated her living room with a lamp and an old record jacket which she bought at the same flea market.

Next we visited Union Square Green Market. Plenty of fresh vegetables, fruits, herbs, dairy products and flowers are put out on tables. These products are brought into Manhattan by farmers from neighboring New Jersey. We could feel autumn in the middle of New York just by looking at the heaps of apples in wooden boxes and beautiful wreaths made of straw and snake gourds. Since the weather was so lovely, we sat on a bench in the Square and enjoyed homemade pumpkin pie and fresh grape juice as a late breakfast.

Suddenly, an old memory came back to Angie. It was when she was here as a child and saw an unusual thing being sold. It was an Osage orange, which looked like a giant head of broccoli. When cut, the inside looked like a kiwi fruit, but she was surprised to hear it was not edible. Actually, it is an insect repellent. I heard that one summer in New York killer mosquitoes scared the people to death. Osage oranges were cut in half and placed in many parts of Central Park to get rid of those mosquitoes.

New York is getting colder these days. I wonder what the weather is like in Japan now.

(379 words)

Notes

▶ **p. 64**
l. 1 **get the best deals** 「もっともお得な値段で買える」
l. 4 **flea market** 「蚤の市」土曜、日曜日になると NY のあちこちで中古の衣服、アクセサリー、家具を並べた市がたつ。特に6番街の 25th St. から 26th St. あたりの広い駐車場を利用した市は有名。
l. 5 **rummage through** 「いろいろあるものからかきわけて探し出す」
l. 5 **stall** 「露店の商品陳列台」
l. 5 **browsing** 「ぶらぶらと見てまわること」
l. 10 **vivid** 「鮮やかな」
l. 11 **faded and smoky** 「色あせてくすんだ」
l. 13 **Union Square Green Market** 「ユニオンスクエア・グリーンマーケット」新鮮な野菜や果物を売る青空市。
l. 16 **heaps of** 「山積みの」

▶ **p. 65**
l. 1 **snake gourds** 「カラスウリ」
l. 5 **Osage orange** 「オサージ・オレンジ」大きくて薄緑色をしている。
l. 7 **edible** 「食べられる」
l. 7 **insect repellent** 「虫除け」

Tips

ユニオンスクエアの市では、手作りパイやマフィンの出店でレシピをもらえる。近くの Union Square Cafe では、この市から取り寄せた新鮮な野菜を使った料理が食べられる。

I Comprehension

次の各文が本文の内容と合っている場合は **T**、間違っている場合は **F** を選びなさい。

1. T / F　Rika bought an antique tin can because the colors on it were a vivid red and blue that she was fond of.

2. T / F　Angie decorated her living room with a lamp and an old record jacket which she bought at the flea market.

3. T / F　What Angie thought was an orange was actually an insect repellent.

II Useful Expressions

（　）の中に適語を入れ、それぞれの和文に合う英文を作りなさい。

1. 私は漫画が好きだが、とくにお気に入りは『ワンピース』だ。
   I love *manga*. (　　　　) (　　　　) (　　　　) (　　　　　　) is *One Piece*.

2. その景色を見た途端、嫌な思い出がよみがえってきた。
   Soon after I saw that scene, a bad memory (　　　　) (　　　　) (　　　　) me.

3. その事件には死ぬほどびっくりした。
   The incident (　　　　　) (　　　　) (　　　　) (　　　　　　).

III Listening

ダイアローグを聞き、空所を埋めなさい。

　　—Rika is at a green market.

Rika: Excuse me, what is this big fruit?

Man: What (　　) (　　　) (　　　　) it is, young lady?

Rika: A kind of melon or broccoli?

Man: This is an insect repellent.

Rika: To kill insects? It's gross.

Man: Do you want (　　　　)?

Rika: No, thanks. (　　　) (　　　　) two apples from over there, please.

Man: Good choice! They are (　　　　) and (　　　　).

Activity

Rika がグリーンマーケットで手に入れたコーン・マフィンのレシピです。下の作り方を読み、正しい順番に並べ替えてみましょう。

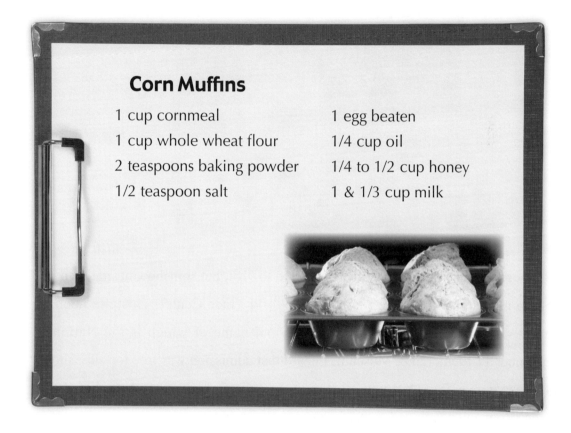

Directions: how to make good corn muffins!

a. Spoon into greased muffin tins.

b. Combine wet ingredients.

c. Bake at 400°F for 20 minutes.

d. Mix wet ingredients with dry ingredients.

e. Combine dry ingredients.

(e) → (　) → (　) → (　) → (　)

UNIT 15 September 11 Memorial

追悼の地を訪れて

Rika's Report

There was one place I had always wanted to visit, but somehow hesitated to do so—up until today. It was the site of the World Trade Center. This afternoon, I finally visited the 9/11 Memorial, the formal name of which is the National September 11 Memorial & Museum. I heard that admission was free for all visitors on Tuesday evenings, but you must sign up online in advance. Actually, there weren't so many people today that I was able to get in without a reservation.

The two deep square pools, North Pool and South Pool, were built in the place where the former Twin Towers were located, to commemorate the victims who were killed in the two terrorist attacks. Nearly three thousand names of those who died on September 11th as well as in the terror attacks in 1993 were engraved in the bronze panels edging the pools. I saw water incessantly falling from the edge of those panels into the large square holes at the bottom of the pools—it felt as if the victims' souls were being absorbed deep down into the ground.

What we saw on TV on September 11th, 2001, has never faded from our memory. The sudden destruction of the two gigantic towers was too tragic an event for us to forget. Many years have passed since then and we cannot recall the event as vividly as we could at that time. But the Memorial and the remains of the attacks—such as the steel frames badly bent in the fire—certainly tell us what actually happened on that day. There are some still-closed buildings around the site, which have remained untouched since the incident.

5   The new tower named One World Trade Center, soon to be completed near the site, will be the tallest building in the city and a new landmark for New Yorkers and tourists. It's a single tower, and unlike the old ones the top of the tower is sharply pointed towards the sky. I wonder with what kind of feelings people will look up to this new icon in New York City...   (350 words)

Notes

▶ p. 68
- *l. 2* **up until today**「今日までずっと」
- *l. 2* **The World Trade Center**「世界貿易センター」ロウアーマンハッタンに位置するビジネス複合施設。
- *l. 5* **sign up online**「ネットで予約する」火曜午後5時から7時までは誰でも無料で入場することができる。それ以外の日時は入場料が必要。
- *l. 5* **in advance**「事前に」
- *l. 8* **Twin Towers**「ツインタワー」世界貿易センター敷地内に1973年に完成したNorth TowerとSouth Tower。2001年9月11日の同時多発テロで崩壊する前までニューヨークで最も高いビルだった。
- *l. 10* **terror attacks in 1993**　1993年2月26日に起きた爆破テロ。死亡者6名の名前が9/11 Memorialに刻まれ追悼されている。
- *l. 13* **absorbed deep down into the ground**「地底深く吸い込まれて」

▶ p. 69
- *l. 3* **still-closed**「いまだに閉鎖されている」
- *l. 5* **One World Trade Center**　世界貿易センター敷地内に建設された高さ1,776フィート（約541メートル）、108階建ての超高層ビル。2014年末に完成予定。
- *l. 9* **icon**「象徴」

Tips

ロウアーマンハッタンと対岸のニュージャージーは、ハドソン川をわたるフェリーか、PATH TRAINという電車で行き来することができ、マンハッタンで働く人々が通勤で利用している。ニュージャージー側のフェリー乗り場近くには、2001年の同時多発テロで殉職した消防士たちの追悼碑がある。

I Comprehension

次の各文が本文の内容と合っている場合は T、間違っている場合は F を選びなさい。

1. T / F   Rika could enter the 9/11 Memorial without a reservation on Tuesday evening.

2. T / F   The Memorial was built to commemorate the victims of the Vietnam War.

3. T / F   One World Trade Center will be the tallest building in New York.

II Useful Expressions

(   ) の中に適語を入れ、それぞれの和文に合う英文を作りなさい。

1. 初めての会合なので、皆の前で発言するのを躊躇した。
   It was the first meeting for me, so I (   ) (   ) speak up in front of everyone.

2. ツアーに参加する場合は、事前に申し込んでください。
   If you want to participate in the tour, please (   ) (   ) in advance.

3. その街はオランダにそっくりで、まるで本物のオランダにいる気分だった。
   The town looks like the Netherlands so much that I felt (   ) (   ) (   ) (   ) really in the Netherlands.

III Listening

ダイアローグを聞き、空所を埋めなさい。

　　—Rika talks to the reception lady at the 9/11 Memorial & Museum.

Rika: Excuse me, but I didn't make a reservation (   ) (   ). Can I enter the Memorial Museum?

Woman: Well, we have (   ) (   ) today, so you don't need a reservation. Please go in.

Rika: Great! Can I have (   ) (   ) (   )?

Woman: Yes, what language do you want?

Rika: Japanese, please. Thank you.

Woman: (   ) (   )!

Activity

September 11 Memorial & Museum での撮影に関する規則事項を読み、下の１～５の文で規則と合っているものには **T**、規則と合っていないものには **F** を（　）に書き入れましょう。

> Inside the Memorial Museum, personal photos, video, and/or audio recordings are permitted for private, noncommercial use only with some exceptions, and in all cases so long as the activity does not impede pedestrian traffic in any way.
>
> a. All camera and/or audio recording equipment, including tripods, are subject to security screening pursuant to Section VI Security Screening and are permissible inside the Memorial Museum at the discretion of 9/11 Memorial & Museum Security Staff.
>
> b. In permitted Memorial Museum areas, personal photography, videography, and audio recording is allowed as long as it does not impede pedestrian traffic or exhibition viewing in any way.
>
> c. The use of a flash is prohibited in all Memorial Museum areas, at all times.

(www.911memorial.org/visitor-rules-and-regulations より抜粋)

1. (　) Taking personal photos is permitted for private, noncommercial use only.
2. (　) Making audio recordings is not permitted for commercial use.
3. (　) Cameras must be checked at the security screening area in the museum.
4. (　) Using tripods is prohibited in the museum.
5. (　) The use of a flash is not permitted in all Memorial Museum areas.

A Japanese in New York [3]

Yuta Takeda
—Sales representative at
 JTB Travel Network Company (JTN)

竹田さんはオーストリアの高校を卒業した後、アリゾナ州立大学でツーリズムを専攻しました。JTN に勤める前は日本のホテルでフロントデスクや接客業務などを経験しました。現在はツアーのアレンジなどの業務に携わっていますが、少しでも多くのお客様に予約してもらうため、さまざまな努力をしています。NY でのお勧めスポットは川沿いの散歩です。自らもサッカーを趣味としていますが、アメリカに来る際には何かひとつでも得意なことがあると強みになると感じています。

英語のナレーションを聞き、1〜5のアンダーラインの箇所に当てはまるものを a〜c の中から選びなさい。

1. He studied _____ at Arizona State University.
   a. tourism   b. business   c. marketing

2. He lived in _____ and the U.S. when he was younger.
   a. Australia   b. Austria   c. Argentina

3. In order to attract more customers, he _____ on a regular basis.
   a. sends them letters   b. calls them directly   c. emails them information

4. In NY, he recommends that you _____.
   a. stroll along the famous rivers   b. visit museums   c. swim at a sports facility

5. He thinks the fact that he is good at playing _____ is an advantage to living in NY.
   a. baseball   b. basketball   c. soccer

Notes

Sakura Hotel 外国人客に人気の格安ホテルチェーン。
devise effective measures 効果的な手段を講じる。
stroll along ... ... 沿いを散歩する。

New Yorkの街角から [3]

――― ベンダー ―――

　ニューヨークの街を歩いていると、通りのいたるところでベンダー（Vendor）と呼ばれる食べ物の屋台を見かける。ニューヨーク市内の屋台の数は、1万とも言われている。

　屋台では、ホットドッグやプレッツェルはもちろん、世界中のさまざまな種類の食べ物が手頃な値段で売られている。飲み物と一緒でも、5ドルから10ドルで買うことができ、外のベンチで座って食べたい時、短い時間で腹ごしらえをしたい時にはとても手軽で、財布にもやさしい。

　こうした屋台の中から、もっとも美味しく人気のある食べ物を売る屋台に与えらえる賞が、The Vendy Cup（最優秀屋台賞）だ。The Vendy Awardsという組織が毎年1回選考イベントを行っており、一般市民によるネット投票で選ばれた20以上の屋台について、飲食業界で実績がある審査員たちが最終選考で評価を決める、というしくみだ。選考会は例年9月に開催される。

　2005年から始まったVendy Awardsで歴代のVendy Cup受賞屋台を見ると、半分以上がメキシコの屋台で、それ以外は、ドイツ、パキスタン、スリランカ、パレスティナの屋台となっている。

　一番人気のメキシコの屋台では、肉や豆、野菜をのせてはさんだタコスが特に人気のようだ。パキスタンの屋台は、イスラム教徒の食事「ハラルフード」のチキン料理、ドイツの屋台はソーセージやミートボール、スリランカの屋台はポテトと生野菜を「ドーサ」（スリランカ風クレープ）で包んだ料理、パレスティナの屋台はスパイシーなチキンがのったライス……それぞれ本場の味を提供している。

　どの屋台がどの場所で開いているかは、newyorkstreetfood.comなどのウェブサイトや、屋台のTwitterで確認することができる。数ある屋台の中から自分のお気に入りの屋台を見つけるのも、ニューヨークならではの楽しみである。

UNIT 16 Central Park & City Marathon

セントラルパークとシティマラソン

Rika's Report

"Don't you just love New York in the fall?" This is the line Meg Ryan said in the movie, *You've Got Mail*. I think the expression just fits Central Park these days. Today, I saw people shooting a film at the Lake. Such shootings are not unusual here since the rustic scenery surrounded by modern buildings makes a perfect
5 setting for movies.

I just recalled what Oliver told me a few days ago. When he was here thirteen years ago and walking near the Lake, he noticed a middle-aged man with gray hair, probably the protagonist, standing in the center of the Bow Bridge. The man was gazing at a beautiful young woman in a boat floating silently on the water. Later he
10 found out they were shooting the movie, *Autumn in New York*— and the guy on the bridge was Richard Gere!

I continued walking on crunchy fallen leaves and my eyes were drawn to those fat, cute squirrels on the lawn. I then noticed many more joggers than usual in the park today. Tomorrow is the first Sunday of November, the day of the New York
15 City Marathon, one of the biggest events in the city. Every street light pole has a flag which guides runners throughout the marathon. People start on the bridge

connecting Staten Island and Brooklyn, run through Brooklyn, Queens, and the Bronx, and then finish in Central Park. This city marathon covers the five boroughs of New York City.

5　　Can you imagine how excited I was to stand on the finish line just a day before the race? I found Tavern on the Green nearby. White tents were erected in front of the restaurant where people were lining up for The Marathon Eve Dinner in the evening. The participants will eat pasta and drink beer to build up energy and relax for the race tomorrow. Such a festive atmosphere really matches this dynamic city.

　　Over thirty thousand people from all over the world run every year. There are
10 also many participants from Japan. I will probably go out to Fifth Avenue tomorrow to cheer on those Japanese runners.

(354 words)

Notes

▶ p. 74

- *l. 2* **You've Got Mail**　映画「ユーガット・メール」チャットで知り合った男女の恋と、NYの巨大書店と小さな街角の本屋がその存在をめぐって対立する話が同時進行する。
- *l. 3* **The Lake**　セントラルパークをW. 72nd St. より入ると、間もなく見える美しい湖。
- *l. 4* **rustic**「田園的でのどかな」
- *l. 4* **make a perfect setting for …**「…にぴったりの場所である」
- *l. 8* **protagonist**「主役」
- *l. 8* **Bow Bridge**「ボウ・ブリッジ」The Lakeにかかる古典的なたたずまいの橋。結婚式や映画撮影によく使われる。
- *l. 12* **crunchy**「サクサクと音を立てる」
- *l. 12* **drawn to …**「…にひかれる」
- *l. 14* **New York City Marathon**「ニューヨーク・シティ・マラソン」毎年11月の第一日曜日に開かれる、市民参加型のマラソンレース。

▶ p. 75

- *l. 1* **Staten Island, Brooklyn, Queens, the Bronx**「スタテン島、ブルックリン、クィーンズ、ブロンクス」マンハッタンと共にNY市を構成する5つの区。(巻頭の地図参照)
- *l. 2* **borough**「NY市の行政地区」
- *l. 5* **Tavern on the Green**「タバーン・オン・ザ・グリーン」セントラルパーク内にある高級レストラン。
- *l. 5* **erected**「設営される」
- *l. 6* **lining up for …**「…を待って並んでいる」
- *l. 8* **festive**「お祭り気分の」
- *l. 11* **cheer on …**「…を応援する」

Tips

NYを舞台にした映画は実に多い。最近では、*Superman Returns* や *Enchanted* (邦題：「魔法にかけれられて」)などにセントラル・パークが登場する。撮影中は、そばでフラッシュをたくとスタッフがすぐ飛んでくるので注意。

I Comprehension

次の各文が本文の内容と合っている場合は **T**、間違っている場合は **F** を選びなさい。

1. T / F   Central Park is often used for film shoots.
2. T / F   Oliver immediately realized the man on the bridge was a famous actor.
3. T / F   The runners get enough calories for the Marathon by eating at Tavern on the Green.

II Useful Expressions

（　）の中に適語を入れ、それぞれの和文に合う英文を作りなさい。

1. 君たちは、お似合いの夫婦になると思うよ。
   I think you two will (　　　　) (　　　　) (　　　　　　　) couple.

2. 小学生の列の中で、面白い帽子を被った子に目が行った。
   In a line of elementary school kids, (　　　　) (　　　　) (　　　　) (　　　　　　)
   (　　　　) a child in a funny hat.

3. 決勝戦で日本のチームを応援するために、大勢のサッカーファンが日本から来た。
   A lot of soccer fans came from Japan to (　　　　　　) (　　　　) the Japanese team at the finals.

III Listening

ダイアローグを聞き、空所を埋めなさい。

—Rika talks to a man in Central Park.

Rika: Do you know (　　　　) (　　　　) they are shooting today?

Man: Sorry, I have (　　　) (　　　　).

Rika: Have you seen any famous movie stars in this park?

Man: Unfortunately, no.

Rika: (　　) (　　　　) (　　) (　　　　) take a photo of Johnny Depp if he were here. I'm a big fan of his.

Man: (　　　) (　　　　　) not to use the flash while they are shooting. You'll be told off.

76

Unit 16

Activity

下の地図とイラストを参考にして、次のa〜eの場所はセントラルパークのどこにあるか、（　）に記号を書き入れましょう。

a. Wollman Memorial Rink
b. The Lake
c. Sheep Meadow
d. Bethesda Fountain
e. Strawberry Fields

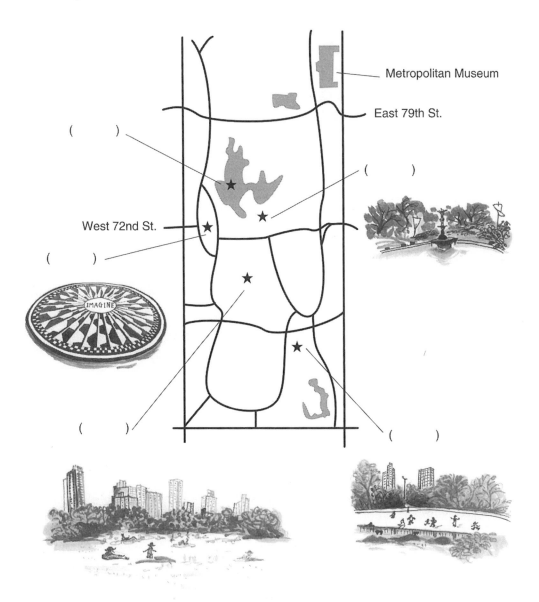

Unit 16　Central Park & City Marathon

UNIT 17 Contemporary Art in New York

ニューヨークは現代美術の宝庫

Rika's Report

You can't talk about Manhattan without mentioning contemporary art. Today I will introduce the Guggenheim Museum and The Museum of Modern Art known as MoMA. Both of them possess a large collection of renowned modern art.

The east side of Central Park is called Museum Mile where various museums
5 are located. Among them, the one that catches your eye with its unique building design is the Guggenheim Museum. Designed by Frank Lloyd Wright, its spiral-cylindrical structure resembles a gigantic snail.

Inside the museum, people walk leisurely up and down the gentle slope of the ramp which continues from the first floor through to the sixth floor. In this structure,
10 visitors do not need to worry about moving from one room to another or watching their feet on the steps like you do in conventional-type museums. Without such distractions, people can concentrate on viewing.

When I visited this museum, there was an exhibition of Japanese avant-garde artists who were active in the 50s and 60s, and their innovative activities called
15 *Gutai* were being introduced. Coming across such Japanese modern art in New York was so fresh and inspiring for me since I hadn't even known of their existence

before coming here.

MoMA, located on 53rd Street in midtown Manhattan, is always crowded with visitors from all over the world. Among the various masterpieces, what impressed me the most was *The Sleeping Gypsy* painted by Henri Rousseau. I had learned about this painting in a high school textbook, but the real *Sleeping Gypsy* stole my heart. A gypsy woman sleeping in the moonlit desert with a lion by her side, serene silence, a clear blue sky at midnight—what a combination and how poetic they are. I was very curious how this masterpiece came into being because Rousseau was extremely poor at the time he painted it.

In MoMA, people look very relaxed and walk freely to see whatever work that interests them. When not viewing the works, people drink coffee in the museum cafe, sunbathe in the courtyard or buy postcards in the Museum Shop. In such an atmosphere, time passes so quickly.

So, when you visit New York, please go to the museums. They will certainly refresh your mind as well as enrich your life. (375 words)

Notes

▶ **p. 78**
- *l. 1* **You can't talk about ... without ...**「... せずに ... は語れない」
- *l. 2* **Guggenheim Museum**「グッゲンハイム美術館」E. 89th St./5th Ave. にあるユニークな外観で有名な美術館。
- *l. 2* **The Museum of Modern Art (MoMA)**「ニューヨーク近代美術館」ミッドタウンに位置し有名な近代美術作品を多数所蔵する美術館。
- *l. 4* **Museum Mile**「ミュージアム・マイル」グッゲンハイム美術館やメトロポリタン美術館など沢山の美術館が立ち並ぶセントラルパーク東側5番街の通称。
- *l. 6* **Frank Lloyd Wright**「フランク・ロイド・ライト」(1867-1959) アメリカの建築家。
- *l. 6* **spiral-cylindrical**「らせん状のスロープが巻きついた円柱型の」
- *l. 9* **ramp**「スロープ」
- *l. 15* ***Gutai***「具体」1950年代から70年代まで関西地区を中心に展開された前衛芸術活動。

▶ **p. 79**
- *l. 4* ***The Sleeping Gypsy***「眠るジプシー女」(1897) アンリ・ルソーの代表作品の1つ。
- *l. 4* **Henri Rousseau**「アンリ・ルソー」(1844-1910) フランスの画家。
- *l. 8* **come into being**「生まれる」

Tips

ミュージアムグッズはNY土産でも人気のひとつである。それぞれの美術館が、ポストカードや所蔵品をモチーフにした文房具や小物、Tシャツなど、そこでしか入手できないデザイン性の高いオリジナル商品を販売している。

I Comprehension

次の各文が本文の内容と合っている場合は **T**、間違っている場合は **F** を選びなさい。

1. T / F　You can find various museums on Museum Mile.
2. T / F　In the Guggenheim Museum, you should be careful while walking because the slopes are steep.
3. T / F　MoMA has a famous painting by Henri Rousseau.

II Useful Expressions

(　) の中に適語を入れ、それぞれの和文に合う英文を作りなさい。

1. 君の話し方は、君のおかあさんによく似ている。
   The way you talk really (　　　　　　) your mother's.

2. もっとも感心したのは、災害後真っ先に、彼がボランティアとして東北へ行ったことだ。
   (　　　) (　　　　　) (　　　) the most was that he went to Tohoku as a volunteer right after the disaster.

3. 森林浴をすると、気分がすがすがしくなりますよ。
   Taking a walk in the woods will certainly (　　　　　) (　　　　　) (　　　　　).

III Listening

ダイアローグを聞き、空所を埋めなさい。

　—Rika and Angie talk about the museums in New York.

Rika:　There're a lot of museums in New York. Do you have any suggestions about which museums (　　) (　　　　) (　　　　)?

Angie:　Well, (　　) (　　　　) (　　　) what kind of art you like.

Rika:　I like contemporary art rather than classical art.

Angie:　Then, the Guggenheim or MoMA could be (　　　) (　　　　) (　　　　　).
　　　　But I can (　　　　　　) the Whitney Museum, too.

Activity

次の1〜5のニューヨークの美術館の特徴を読み、それぞれに当てはまる美術館を下の地図から選んで名前を（　）の中に書き入れましょう。

1. (　　　　　　　) is facing Fifth Avenue and famous for early 20th-century German and Austrian art.

2. (　　　　　　　) is on 53rd St. and mainly houses a collection of 20th century art.

3. (　　　　　　　) is in Central Park and one of the four biggest museums in the world.

4. (　　　　　　　), which was designed by Frank Lloyd Wright, is to the north of the Metropolitan Museum.

5. (　　　　　　　) is a small museum which houses a large Renaissance collection.

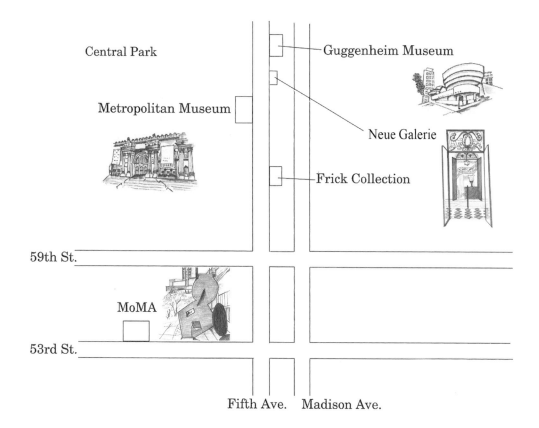

UNIT 18 Christmas in New York

ニューヨークのクリスマス

Rika's Report

It is the time of year to send and receive letters and emails starting with "Dear Family" or "Hi Friends." People in New York are already in the Christmas mood and I am getting excited, too.

Angie and I took a walk downtown today. First, we went to the Rockefeller Center to see the famous Christmas tree. The Tree Lighting Ceremony is always held in the first week of December.

The whole view was so enchanting! In the short pathway from Fifth Avenue to the GE Building, white angel decorations were shining. School children in reindeer hats were marching with beaming smiles. Beyond them people were gliding across the huge skating rink with the gigantic tree and the shimmering Prometheus statue in the background. You can see such a scene in the last scene of *Home Alone 2*.

We strolled along Fifth Avenue for a while and saw some nice and unique decorations on the buildings. Cartier was tied up with a giant ribbon which made the whole building look like a present, and Saks Fifth Avenue had a line of mini trees in the windows. To be honest, Christmas in New York is somewhat different than what I had thought it was before coming here. It is not an all-town festival in which people make a gleeful racket, but rather it is a time for families and friends to get together, feeling warm and cozy in their own homes.

The climax of the day was *The Nutcracker* performed at the New York State Theater where we met Oliver and Sara. There was also a beautiful Christmas tree near the fountain in the center of Lincoln Center. Many people, all dressed up under their coats, were already lining up at the entrance and swapping jokes and stories. I noticed some elderly people accompanying neatly-dressed children. Oliver said, "My parents used to bring me and my sister here every Christmas. If you are a New Yorker, you can't miss the NYCB's *Nutcracker*." I fully understood his comment after the show. Balanchine's unique choreography, the dazzling corps de ballet and the children selected by audition for this particular performance were absolutely fantastic!

I hope people in Japan are enjoying this festive season as well.　　　(370 words)

Notes

▶ **p. 82**
- *l. 8* **GE Building**「GEビル」ロックフェラー・センターの中心に立つ70階建てのビル。中にNBCスタジオがあり、見学できる。
- *l. 9* **beaming smiles**「溢れるような笑顔」
- *l. 9* **glide across ...**「…を滑る」
- *l. 10* **shimmering**「きらきら光る」
- *l. 10* **Prometheus statue**「プロメテウスの像」
- *l. 13* **Cartier**「カルティエ」高級ブランドの1つ。
- *l. 14* **Saks Fifth Avenue**「サックス・フィフス・アベニュー」高級デパートの1つ。
- *l. 16* **all-town festival**「街全体で祝う祭り」

▶ **p. 83**
- *l. 1* **make a gleeful racket**「嬉しくて大はしゃぎをする」
- *l. 3* ***The Nutcracker***（バレエの）「くるみ割り人形」
- *l. 3* **New York State Theater**「ニューヨーク州立劇場」
- *l. 9* **NYCB**「ニューヨーク・シティ・バレエ」
- *l. 10* **Balanchine**「ジョージ・バランシン」(1904-1983) ロシア出身で、アメリカが誇る振付家。
- *l. 10* **choreography**「振り付け」
- *l. 10* **corps de ballet**「群舞」

映画 *Home Alone 2* では、母と子が最後にロックフェラー・センターの巨大なツリーとスケートリンクの前で再会する。点灯式の様子は、毎年日本でも放映される。

I Comprehension

次の各文が本文の内容と合っている場合は T、間違っている場合は F を選びなさい。

1. T / F　The Rockefeller Center's Tree Lighting Ceremony is held in the first week of December.
2. T / F　You can see some nicely decorated buildings on Fifth Avenue in the Christmas season.
3. T / F　Oliver used to see *The Nutcracker* with his grandparents every year.

II Useful Expressions

(　) の中に適語を入れ、それぞれの和文に合う英文を作りなさい。

1. いよいよこの時期は、4年生が就職活動を始める時だね。
   (　　) (　　) (　　　) (　　) (　　　　) when every senior starts job-hunting.

2. パーティであまり大騒ぎするなよ。
   Don't (　　　) (　　) (　　　　) at the party!

3. 父は、週末になるとよく映画に連れていってくれた。
   My father (　　　) (　　) (　　　) me to a movie every weekend.

III Listening

ダイアローグを聞き、空所を埋めなさい。

　　—Rika and Sara talk about Christmas.

Rika: (　　　) (　　) (　　　) (　　　) (　　　　) Christmas holidays, Sara?

Sara: I usually go back to my hometown in Boston and spend time with my family. All my relatives gather at my parents' place.

Rika: Do you exchange presents?

Sara: Yeah, it's a lot of work to (　　　) (　　) (　　　) (　　　　) for everybody. But I found a good one for my sister, today.

Rika: What is it?

Sara: An NYCB magnet puzzle. I'm sure she'll (　　　) (　　　).

Unit 18

Activity

Rika からクリスマスカードが送られてきたと想定し、左上の差出人の書き方を参考にして、自分の宛名と住所を封筒に書いてみましょう。

Rika Tanaka
159 West 15th St.
NY 10011
USA

STAMP

_____
_____
_____
_____
Japan   VIA AIRMAIL

UNIT 19 Email from the Teacher (2)

ニューヨークへのメッセージ (2)

Dear Rika,

Thank you for reporting on Christmas in New York. I'm glad to hear that you spent such an enjoyable time before finishing your ten-month stay and coming back to Japan early next year. How are you feeling now?

5   Over these several months, I've been very impressed with your reports. You have a positive attitude toward everything and actively engage in whatever interests you. You are not only studying hard, but also trying to know more about the city and the people around you.

I can see from your reports that the Green Market and Central Park
10 serve as a good oasis for busy New Yorkers who are surrounded by mammoth buildings. Going to musicals or museums seems to be a part of their lives, not something particularly special. For many art and music lovers, it's a place where one can be in touch with both classical and contemporary arts and enjoy world-famous performances as a part
15 of daily life.

As for the dark side of the city, it has suffered several terrorist attacks in the past. I still clearly remember the Twin Towers which used be a landmark for New Yorkers and tourists. The city has engraved those tragic events on various monuments, trying to remember the people who lost their lives in the events and to console those who lost their beloved ones.

By the way, did you know that Tokyo Station has recently been renovated as well? It marked its centennial in 2014 and a lot of visitors have been coming to see the newly renovated station. Both Grand Central Terminal and Tokyo Station have a theme in common: "Utilization for the next 100 years," and I find many similarities between New York and Tokyo. One of them is that they look positively into the future and keep energetically evolving. I hope these two cities will continue to develop together as good rivals.

Well, your stay in New York is going to finish soon. I hope you fully enjoy your remaining time in New York. I look forward to hearing more about the city when you come back.

See you soon in Tokyo!

Best always,
May J. Sato

(361 words)

Notes

▶ **p. 86**
- l. 6 **actively engage in ...**「... に積極的に関わる」
- l. 10 **serve as a good oasis**「ほっとするオアシスのような役割を果たす」
- l. 11 **mammoth buildings**「超高層ビル」
- l. 13 **be in touch with ...**「... に接する」

▶ **p. 87**
- l. 6 **mark its centennial**「100 周年を祝う」
- l. 8 **have a theme in common**「共通するテーマを持つ」
- l. 8 **"Utilization for the next 100 years"**「次の 100 年に向けた活用」
- l. 10 **look positively into the future**「未来を前向きに見据える」
- l. 11 **keep energetically evolving**「エネルギッシュに進化し続ける」

Eメールの書き方 ❷

ライティングクラスの宿題のために、Rika がグランドセントラル駅の広報担当 Jones さんに書いたメールです。誰かに何か依頼するメールの書き方を学びましょう。

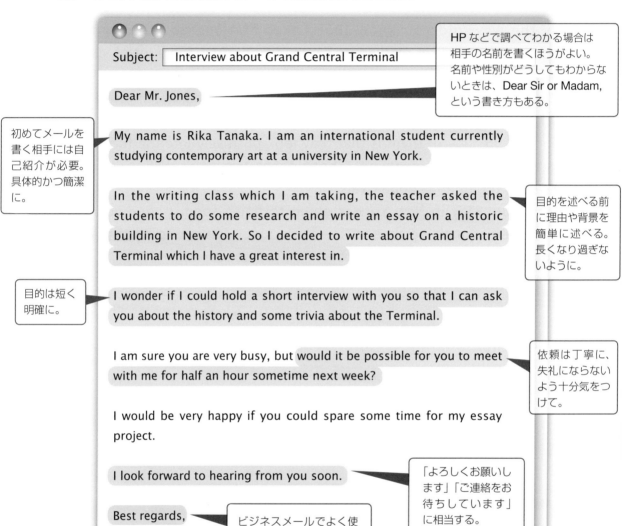

NOTES

currently studying ...「現在 ... を勉強中である」
do some research (on) 「(... について) リサーチする」
I wonder if I could ...「... をお願いできるでしょうか」(仮定法)
hold an interview with ...「... を相手にインタビュー取材をする」
trivia 「ちょっとした裏話」
sometime next week 「来週のいつか」
I would be very happy if you could ...「... してくれたら嬉しい」(仮定法)
spare some time for ...「... のために時間を割く」

Unit 19

Activity   Eメールを書いてみましょう❷

NYにあるギャラリーの広報担当者に取材申し込みのメールを書いてみましょう。

Subject: _____

_____

関連表現

● 何かについて依頼をする

I would be very happy to get your feedback on my essay.（私のエッセイに感想をいただけると幸いです）

Could you please send me more information about the orientation?（オリエンテーションについてもう少し情報を送っていただけますか？）

Would you please forward this email to Mr. Jones?（ジョーンズ氏にこのメールを転送していただけますか？）

● 感謝の気持ちを表す（通常、文末に書くことが多い）

Thank you for your cooperation.（ご協力ありがとうございます）

I really appreciate your help.（助けていただき、とても感謝しています）

Thank you in advance.（よろしくお願いします）＊先に礼を言う場合

Thank you always.（いつもありがとうございます）＊結句として

メール作成上の注意点

◎ 依頼の理由や目的は、相手がすぐ気がつくように、メールの始めの方に書こう。
◎ 依頼するときは丁寧に。**would/could** などの助動詞や **please** を使うことによって丁寧に聞こえる。
◎ 相手への感謝の文言を忘れずに。

UNIT 20 Goodbye, New York

さよなら、ニューヨーク！

Rika's Report

This will be my last report from New York. I am returning to Japan in a week. I have been a bit down and emotional these days. Every time I see my friends to say goodbye or go back to places I once visited, I cannot hold back my tears. Because I *love* New York.

5　Have you ever seen the sign, "I LOVE NEW YORK" in which "LOVE" is a heart mark? This campaign logo was a call for the revival of New York and was designed two years after the Vietnam War ended. People at that time were suffering from a financial crisis, soaring crime, deterioration of the city landscape, all of which caused a rapid decrease in the number of tourists. But the campaign was
10　successful and the city revived. This is because New Yorkers love their city. They united together to bring the charm and energy back into the city.

Although my experience in New York has been just ten months, I never felt that I was a foreigner here. Taxi drivers, employees at restaurants, and international students at school often spoke English with a heavy accent. But one thing people
15　living in New York have in common, whether they are American nationals or immigrants, is that they are certain of what they want to achieve here. Some work

in hotel kitchens to send money to their families. Some wait on tables, while studying at a school to be actors or actresses and dreaming of becoming a star someday. Without a strong identity and a sense of acheivement, one would find it difficult to survive in this diverse city.

5   Yesterday my friends at the dorm threw a farewell party for me. Tonight, I visited Oliver and Sara with Angie and Jonathan to say goodbye. They all hugged me tightly and said, "We'll all miss you. You have to come back here again." I could hardly suppress my emotions and my eyes were full of tears. "How can I forget New York and the time I spent with you?"

10   I assure you I will come back to this city someday and shout out in a loud voice, "I LOVE NEW YORK!" Goodbye, New York! Goodbye, dear friends!

(369 words)

Notes

▶ p. 90
- l. 2 **down**「憂鬱な気分でいる」
- l. 3 **hold back**「抑える」
- l. 8 **soaring**「急増する」
- l. 8 **deterioration**「悪化」
- l. 15 **American national**「米国籍を持ったアメリカ人」
- l. 16 **certain of ...**「...についてしっかりとした考えを持っている」

▶ p. 91
- l. 1 **wait on tables**「給仕をする」アメリカでは各テーブルごとに係が決まっており、専任で世話をする。
- l. 3 **a sense of achievement**「達成感」
- l. 5 **threw a farewell party**「送別会をしてくれた」
- l. 8 **suppress**「抑える」

Tips

NYは移民が多く、人種もさまざまである。街中で正統派の英語を聞くことは珍しい。ファースト・フードの店では、こちらが注文したものと違う中身のサンドイッチが出てくることもしばしばである。ゆえに英語が苦手でも堂々と渡り合えばよい。言語と文化の壁を超えた空間がNYにはあり、それが世界中の人々を惹きつけている。

I Comprehension

次の各文が本文の内容と合っている場合は **T**、間違っている場合は **F** を選びなさい。

1. T / F　Rika is sad because she has to leave NY in a week.
2. T / F　You need to have a strong identity and a sense of achievement to survive in New York.
3. T / F　Rika regrets that she could not make many friends while she was in NY.

II Useful Expressions

(　) の中に適語を入れ、それぞれの和文に合う英文を作りなさい。

1. その映画を見るたびに、泣かずにはいられません。
   (　　　　) (　　　　) I see that movie, I can't stop crying.

2. 我々に共通するのは、2人ともビートルズが好きなことです。
   One thing we have (　　　) (　　　　　) is that we both like the Beatles.

3. 友だちが、誕生日にサプライズパーティをしてくれました。
   My friends (　　　　) (　　　) (　　　　　) (　　　　) for my birthday.

III Listening

ダイアローグを聞き、空所を埋めなさい。

　　—Rika talks with Oliver and Sara at the farewell party for her.

Oliver:　When are you (　　　　) (　　) Tokyo?
Rika:　Next Monday.
Sara:　We'll (　　　) (　　　　) you. Will you email us?
Rika:　Sure. We can talk on Skype, too.
Oliver:　Let's all (　　　) (　　) (　　　　).
Rika:　Thank you for (　　　　　). You were always so helpful.
Sara:　You're welcome.
Oliver:　(　　　) (　　　　). Enjoy the rest of your university life in Japan.

Unit 20

Activity

ニューヨークで行われる１年間の行事を調べ、行事が行われる月を（　）に記入しましょう。

NY CITY CALENDAR OF EVENTS

(1) New Year's Day

(   ) Macy's Fireworks Display (for Independence Day)

(   ) Halloween Parade

(   ) New York City Marathon

(3) St. Patrick's Day Parade

(   ) Gay and Lesbian Pride Day Parade (June)

(   ) Easter Parade

(   ) Five Boro Bike Tour (first Sunday in May)

(9) Labor Day Parade (first Monday in September)

(   ) U.S. Open (starting in August)

(   ) Black History Month (February)

(12) Christmas Tree Lighting Ceremony

A Japanese in New York [4]

Masayo Hosono
—Operation representative at
JTB Travel Network Company (JTN)

細野さんはNYの州立大学を卒業したあと、JTNで働きはじめました。最初は英語とメイクの勉強をするためにアメリカに来ましたが、日本のホスピタリティの質の高さに気づき、旅行業に進むことを決めました。JTNでは主にツアーの手配をてがけています。5年間半ほどアメリカに住むと、日本人の食や文化、言語そのものに改めて魅力を感じ、日本語の本をよく読んでいます。休みの日はNY市内の公園で、空を見上げながら音楽を聴いたり、本を読んだりしています。

英語のナレーションを聞き、1～5のアンダーラインの箇所に当てはまるものをa～cの中から選びなさい。

1. She came to the U.S. with the aim of studying _____.
   a. fashion design　　b. makeup artistry　　c. visual art

2. She found hospitality services in Japan are _____ those in the U.S.
   a. not so good as　　b. better than　　c. not much different from

3. She has read _____ Japanese books since she came to the U.S.
   a. only few　　b. a few　　c. many

4. In Central Park and Bryant Park, she enjoys _____, listening to music, and reading books.
   a. eating food　　b. sunbathing　　c. jogging

5. In the U.S., you should _____ about what you don't want or don't agree with.
   a. keep silent　　b. ask for someone's opinion　　c. clearly say "no"

Notes

has a stronger attachment to ... ... に対して以前より強い愛着を感じる。
Central Park セントラルパーク。Unit 16 を参照。
Bryant Park ブライアントパーク。Unit 3 と同章 Notes を参照。

New Yorkの街角から [4]

——**NYでスポーツ観戦！**——

　メジャーリーグのヤンキースとメッツ、バスケットボールのニックスとブルックリン・ネッツ、アイスホッケーのレンジャーズとアイランダーズ……これらはすべて、ニューヨークを根拠地にしているプロスポーツチームだ。

　メジャーリーグは、日本人選手の活躍でますます身近な話題になり、NBA（National Basketball Association）の人気チームの試合は、衛星放送で中継される。ニューヨークでプロの白熱した試合を生で見ることができたら、どんなにすごいことだろう。

　バスケットボールはとても人気があり、チケットの入手は困難だ。お目当ての日にお目当てのチームの試合を観戦しようとすれば、かなり前にネットで購入するか、旅行代理店に依頼するかしないとむずかしい。

　試合観戦が無理なら、マディソンスクエアガーデンの代わりに、マンハッタンの5番街沿いにあるNBAストアに行ってみよう。店内にはスタープレーヤーたちのポスターが飾られ、試合の生中継を放送している時もある。NBAすべてのチームの名前とロゴが入ったTシャツがずらりと並んでおり、それぞれのチームカラーやロゴマークを見ているだけでも楽しくなる。日本では買うことができないTシャツやグッズは、お土産にもよい。

　野球については、MLB（Major League Baseball）のウェブサイトで当日でもチケットを購入することが可能である。けれども、ヤンキースの試合を地元ヤンキースタジアムで見ようとすると、他のチームの他の球場での試合よりもチケットの値段が3倍以上することがある。それに比べてメッツの方の試合は、席を選ばなければ20ドルで見ることができて手頃である。クイーンズにあるシティフィールド球場でメッツの試合を見ながら、メジャーリーグ観戦の雰囲気を楽しもう。

著者
光藤京子（みつふじ　きょうこ）日英翻訳グループ TAS 代表、翻訳コンサルタント
上杉恵美（うえすぎ　めぐみ）明海大学准教授

《取材協力》
遠藤梨世、佐野健一郎、竹田雄太、細野雅世、土江亨、長尾春花、上杉るい

マイ・ニューヨーク・スケッチブック
［バージョン2］

2015 年 2 月 20 日　第 1 版発行
2023 年 2 月 20 日　第 3 版発行

著　者——光藤京子／上杉恵美
発行者——前田俊秀
発行所——株式会社　三修社
　　　　　〒 150-0001
　　　　　東京都渋谷区神宮前 2-2-22
　　　　　TEL 03-3405-4511 / FAX 03-3405-4522
　　　　　振替 00190-9-72758
　　　　　https://www.sanshusha.co.jp
　　　　　編集担当　三井るり子

印刷所——日経印刷株式会社

© 2015 Printed in Japan　ISBN978-4-384-33444-9 C1082

英文校正 —— 高木エリン
本文 DTP —— Studio A
本文イラスト —— 並木昌子
表紙デザイン —— 峯岸孝之
表紙イラスト —— 松本沙希
準拠 CD 録音 —— ELEC
準拠 CD 制作 —— 高速録音株式会社

JCOPY〈出版者著作権管理機構　委託出版物〉
本書の無断複製は著作権法上での例外を除き禁じられています。複製される場合は、そのつど事前に、出版者著作権管理機構（電話 03-5244-5088 FAX 03-5244-5089 e-mail: info@jcopy.or.jp）の許諾を得てください。